The Fighting 14th

The Fighting 14th
The 14th (Duchess of York's Own) Light Dragoons During the West Indies Campaign, The Peninsular War and The War of 1812
1792-1820

Henry Blackburne Hamilton

LEONAUR

The Fighting 14th
The 14th (Duchess of York's Own) Light Dragoons During the West Indies Campaign, The Peninsular War and The War of 1812
1792-1820
by Henry Blackburne Hamilton

FIRST EDITION

Leonaur is an imprint of Oakpast Ltd
Copyright in this form © 2013 Oakpast Ltd

ISBN: 978-1-78282-213-4 (hardcover)
ISBN: 978-1-78282-214-1 (softcover)

http://www.leonaur.com

Publisher's Notes

The views expressed in this book are not necessarily those of the publisher.

Contents

Historical Record of the 14th Light Dragoons from 1792 7

Historical Record of the 14th Light Dragoons from 1792

This was the time of the French Revolution, and the spirit of republicanism had spread to the French West Indian Islands, where the blacks rose against the planters, committing acts of outrage and spoliation.

1792

The regiment was reviewed in the Phoenix Park, Dublin, on 15th May, by Major-General Richard Whyte. The regimental code was still in use, and each officer had a copy. The chaplain was still on leave, being 70 years of age, and the Reverend Mr. Devereux officiated for him.

Seventeen privates were drafted to Jamaica. In June the regiment moved to Kilkenny, thence in July to Tallow, County Waterford, till November, and thence to Cappoquin in December.

1793

A British Army under the Duke of York went to Flanders to act against the French, and British aid was also given to the planters in St. Domingo (Hayti). During this year the regiment seems to have been frequently on the move, and quartered in turn at Tallow, Cappoquin, Clogheen, and Kilkenny, sending other troops on detachment elsewhere.

1794

In January the headquarters of the regiment were at Clogheen. In March a move was made to Bandon and out-stations, and in September to Clonmel.

Major Arthur Carter received the brevet rank of Lieutenant-Colonel on 1st March, and Colonel Grice Blakeney became Major-General on 3rd October.

Two troops were sent from Ireland to Flanders, and were there attached to the 8th Light Dragoons on arrival. In the muster-roll of these two troops from June to December 1794, they are shown as being in Major-General Vyse's brigade of the army in Flanders. They formed part of the van of the forces under Lieutenant-General the Earl of Moira, which proceeded on the march from Ostend to join the army under His Royal Highness the Duke of York.

The two troops wintered in Holland, taking part in several encounters with the enemy, and after an unusually severe season and a hard campaign, in which several men and six horses were lost, came to Germany early in the following year (1795), and became incorporated with the 8th Regiment of Light Dragoons.

These troops saw a good deal of service. It was on 15th September 1794 that Lieutenant-General Abercromby (under the orders of the Duke of York) marched with the reserve to try and regain the lost position of Boxtell in Brabant, near the River Dommel and the town of Berlicon. He found the enemy so strong that he was obliged to retire, and consequently the Duke of York had to fall back with his army across the Meuse,[1] taking up a position near the old lines of Velpen, three miles in front of Grave. Next day, having crossed the Meuse, he encamped at Wichen, seven miles distant. In the engagement at Boxtell nearly 1500 men were lost, mostly German troops. The squadron of the 14th Light Dragoons lost 2 men who were reported 'missing.' The Battle of Boxtell took place on the 14th September 1794: it was undoubtedly a victory of the French over the allied British and Dutch forces under the Duke of York.

On 6th December 1794 the Duke of York left the army in Holland, and the command of the allied army was taken over by General Walmoden, and of the British by Lieutenant-General Abercromby. In the month of December the troops suffered in-

---

1. Or 'Maas.'

tensely from the inclemency of the weather during the time they were at Grave on the Meuse, near Nimeguen, in Dutch Brabant. The ice was so strong that cavalry and heavy cannon could cross the rivers.

The winter clothing for the men came from Arnheim on the River Rhine. In the action of Tuyl, fought on 30th December, the allies were victorious and drove the enemy across the Waal River. There were no casualties among the cavalry, but the 19th, 33rd, 42nd, 78th, and 80th Regiments, as well as the 'Loyal Emigrants,' lost between them 2 officers and 24 men.

1795

On 5th January, at Geldermalsen, where the enemy was defeated with a loss of 200 men, our losses were 4 officers, 64 men, and 11 horses, which included 7 men and 3 horses of the 11th Light Dragoons; but it does not appear that any losses were incurred by the 14th Light Dragoons or 8th Light Dragoons on this occasion, as the cavalry was mostly in reserve.

On the 8th January, at a place near Bueren, on the River Lingen, a battle took place. The British and allies were opposed to very superior forces of the enemy, but fought with the greatest gallantry, and lost 3 officers and 18 men killed, 8 officers, 113 men, and 3 horses wounded. No casualties occurred among the cavalry. On this occasion Major-General Lord Cathcart was in command. The 27th and 28th Regiments suffered heavily, and we had to retire across the Lingen to Elst.

Another engagement took place here on 10th January, when the British lost several officers and men. Lieutenant-General Abercromby, who was marching on Echlade, suddenly found himself threatened by the French both on his left flank and in rear, the Hanoverians and Austrians being also hard pressed by bodies of the enemy. In this state of affairs Lieutenant-General Abercromby retreated across the Lech, and eventually the whole British Army had to retire into Westphalia and Germany, suffering great hardships and privations on their march. They reached Deventer on 14th January, thence proceeding to Loonen and other places in Guelderland, and by the month of March General Abercromby had established the headquarters of the British

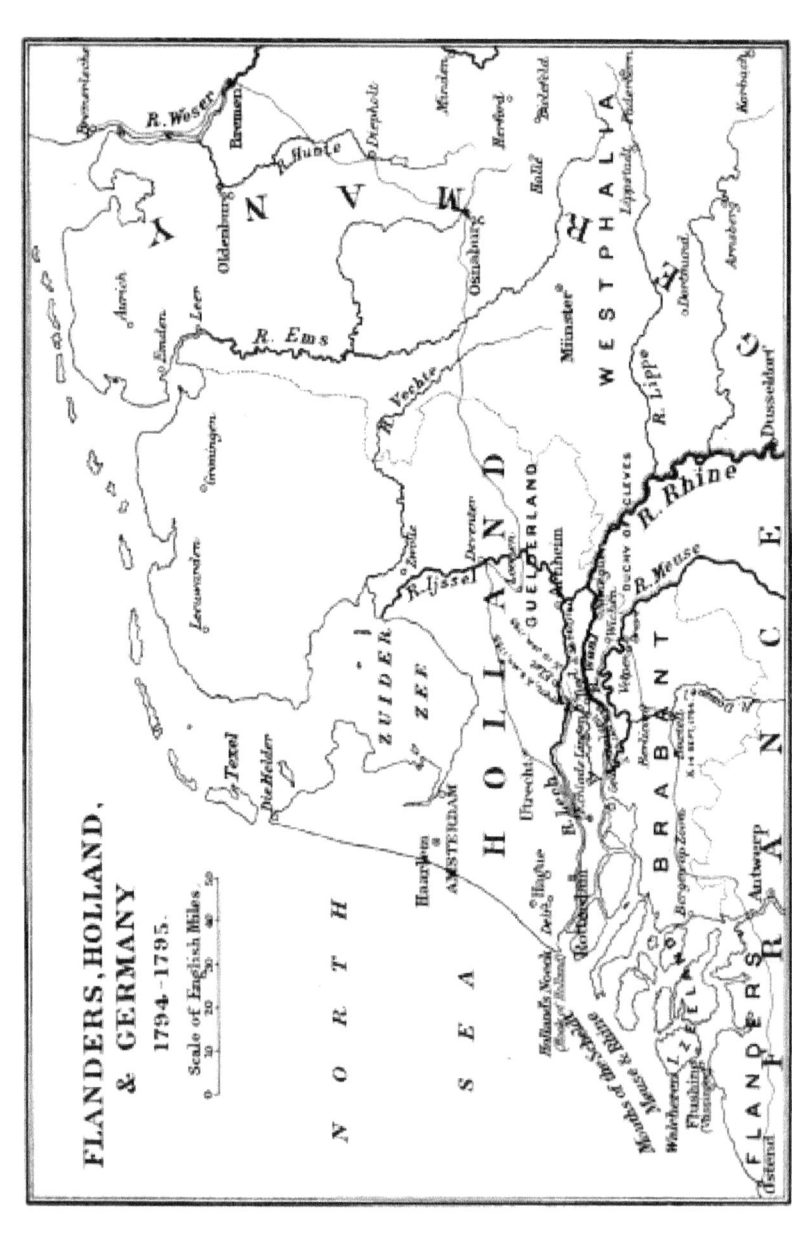

troops at Osnaburg, and later at Diephelt in Westphalia.

Towards the end of March the British marched to Bremen on Weser, and on the 14th April 1795 a large force embarked at Bremerleche, leaving for a time Major-General D. Dundas and Lord Cathcart with a detachment of artillery and the whole of the British cavalry, whilst the remainder sailed for England on the 24th April. In this campaign the superior forces of the enemy completely overpowered the British and their allies. [2]

The two troops of the 14th Light Dragoons which took part in these operations were by this time incorporated with the 8th Light Dragoons, now the 8th King's Royal Irish Hussars, and so we take leave of them to return to the main body of the regiment which we left in Ireland in County Tipperary.

For some years the spirit of republicanism had run riot in the French West Indian Islands, and numerous acts of outrage and spoliation had been committed by the blacks who had hitherto been slaves, against the properties of their owners. In 1793 the planters of St. Domingo obtained British aid, whilst the revolutionists afterwards received assistance from France. At this period the 7 troops of the Fourteenth at Clonmel were ordered out to St. Domingo. The establishment at this time was 450 rank and file, with 486 troop-horses.

The 7 troops gave up their horses to the 24th Light Dragoons at Clonmel, and in June embarked without horses at Waterford under the superintendence of Major-General John William Egerton, whence they sailed to Bristol, taking with them their appointments and everything ready for service. They subsequently proceeded to Hayti or St. Domingo, one of the Leeward Islands in the Atlantic, for service there under Brevet Lieutenant-Colonel A. Carter. At Bristol the regiment met the 13th Light Dragoons destined for the same service as themselves, also the 30th Light Dragoons under Colonel Sir John Garden, as well as the 32nd Light Dragoons under Colonel Blake. The two latter regiments were mounted, and had come from Ireland to do duty in England. Those regiments destined for active service,

---

2. The above is taken from Jones's *Historical Journal of the British Campaign on the Continent with the retreat through Holland, 1794-95* (published 1797).

after landing at Bristol were stationed in billets in the adjacent towns, till the vessels which were to convey them to the West Indies were ready to receive them.

On arrival at St. Domingo the regiment was supplied with horses from America, and was soon engaged in active operations against the bands of armed negroes and mulattoes who had enrolled themselves under the banners of the French Republic. During the years 1795, 1796, and 1797, numerous actions occurred, but against a hundred thousand trained blacks who had been instructed in European discipline, the few British troops on the island were unable to do more than exhibit many examples of discipline and valour.[3]

1796

There was a small party of the regiment stationed at Marlborough in England, and a depot at Maidstone, and the establishments of men and horses were largely augmented, but the effectives were very far below these numbers, owing to the casualties on service and want of recruits.

The country of Hayti or St. Domingo was close and hilly, and therefore quite unsuited to cavalry operations; the climate, moreover, was unhealthy in the extreme, and after a time yellow fever broke out, and made fearful ravages amongst the British forces. There were seven cavalry regiments serving in the expedition, *viz.* the 13th, 14th, 17th, 18th, 21st, 26th, and 29th Light Dragoons, and these suffered most terribly from the fatal scourge. The deaths were so numerous and rapid that regiments could not bury their own dead, and it is recorded that the 13th Light Dragoons had to obtain help in this duty from the men of the 56th Regiment serving near them. A vivid picture of the state of affairs is given in the early pages of Gleig's *Hussar*, published in 1837.[4]

There is an old parchment muster-roll of the 14th Light Dragoons now preserved in the Public Record Office, Chancery Lane, London, dated May to December 1795, in which

---

3. Cannon's *Record*.
4. *The Hussar* by Norbert Landsheit & G. R. Gleig and *The Subaltern* by George Robert Gleig are also published by Leonaur.

Major Arthur Carter and four privates are returned as 'Prisoners of War,' a few men are returned as 'at Halstead,' and others as 'in England.' This muster-roll was sworn to by Major (Brevet Lieutenant-Colonel) Sir J. Dunbar, Bart., on the 26th April 1798, at Marylebone, before a justice of the peace. In the old 'Monthly Returns,' also preserved in the Public Record Office, the 14th Light Dragoons on 1st July 1795 are accounted for as follows:—

Seven Troops at Maryborough.
Two Troops on foreign service. (108 Horses)

And the nine Troops are thus designated:—

The Colonel's (Lieutenant-General R. Sloper's).
The Lieutenant-Colonel's (Major-General Grice Blakeney's).
The Major's (Brevet Lieutenant-Colonel Arthur Carter's on foreign service).
Captain the Honourable James Butler's (on leave).
Captain N. Hutchinson's.
Captain Hamilton Gorge's.
Captain Henry Browne's.
Captain G. H. Montgomery's.
——— vacant (afterwards Captain J. Kearnay's).

Probably this return had reference to the period just before the seven troops from Ireland embarked in the south of England for the West Indies, and when they were on their way to the coast. It is probable Lieutenant-Colonel Carter with some other officers and part of a troop proceeded early in the year 1795 to St. Domingo, and was followed by the remainder of the regiment in July or later. Colonel Blakeney having been promoted Major-General before the regiment embarked, was practically succeeded in command by Lieutenant-Colonel Carter, the senior major, and Captain Sir J. Dunbar, Bart., had been promoted Major on augmentation, on 1st September 1795.

On the 3rd May, Lieutenant-General Sir Robert Sloper became General.

1797

Cannon relates that in an enterprise against the post of 'Le Mirebalais' a town to the north of Port-au-Prince on the west coast of St. Domingo, a detachment of the 14th, 18th, and 21st Light Dragoons, commanded by Brevet Lieutenant-Colonel Arthur Carter of the 14th Light Dragoons, distinguished itself, and was commended in the public despatches.

The bulletins of 1797-98 contain the following relative to the affair at Mirebalais:—

Despatch of Brigadier-General Churchill to Lieutenant-General George Simcox, commanding His Majesty's troops in the Isle of St. Domingo, dated Mirebalais, June 2nd, 1797.

We were enabled to drive the enemy from a very advantageous position they had taken, which, from their superiority of numbers (about 1200 men), with three pieces of cannon, must in all probability have cost us a number of valuable lives to have carried; but this additional strength [5] gave us an easy victory, for no sooner did they perceive a detachment of infantry and cavalry which I sent to guard the heights and turn their right flank, than they immediately fled in the utmost confusion, and with such precipitation, that though Lieutenant-Colonel Carter with the detachments of the 14th, 18th, and 21st Dragoons pursued them with that alacrity and spirit which has ever distinguished him, he could only come up with a very few.

He succeeded, however, in driving a great many into the River Artibonite, most of whom perished, and he had the good fortune to take two of the guns with their ammunition, mules, etc. etc. The third gun was most probably lost in the river, the carriage being left behind. We found the fort in the Bourg of Mirebalais as perfect as it had ever been and in no manner destroyed. I enclose a return of the artillery and ammunition found in the fort of Mirebalais, and I am happy to inform your Excellency that the repossession of this important post and district was effected

---

5. This refers to the junction of a column under Colonel Dessources at Port Michell on the previous day.

without loss, one sergeant and one private of the dragoons being all our wounded.

Return of Ordnance and Ordnance stores taken in the fort of Mirebalais on the 2nd June 1797.

2 French 8-pounders badly spiked (since unspiked and rendered serviceable).

2 6-pounders, serviceable. 2 2-pounders, serviceable.

A large proportion of shot for the above ordnance of every description.

The ammunition not ascertained, but stated to be damaged.

    (Signed)   Geo. Churchill, Brigadier-General

The pestilential climate of the West Indies was highly injurious to the health of Europeans, and the 14th Light Dragoons, like other regiments serving there, were soon reduced to a skeleton. When the order came to return home, those who survived were permitted to volunteer into other corps remaining out longer, and those who remained in the regiment, twenty-five in number, were embarked for England, where they arrived in October, and were stationed at Chelmsford.

On the 1st June, General Sir Robert Sloper, K.B., was removed to the Colonelcy of the 4th Dragoons, and Major-General John William Egerton (afterwards Earl of Bridgewater) was appointed to the Colonelcy of the 14th Light Dragoons, from the first Lieutenant-Colonelcy of the 7th Light Dragoons. Major-General Egerton was employed on the staff at Chelmsford when the remnant of the 14th Light Dragoons arrived there from Hayti or St. Domingo, and receiving eight old and worn-out horses with the recruits from the depot at Maidstone, he had the satisfaction soon after of mounting the regiment afresh, and of seeing it within a few years with upwards of 900 horses in its ranks.

There do not appear to be any authentic returns of the actual numbers of the 14th Light Dragoons who embarked for the West Indies, or of those who subsequently returned to England; but in the case of the 13th Light Dragoons there is a very accurate casualty return preserved, and this may be taken as a fair sample of what the casualties of the 14th Light Dragoons probably were in the same campaign, for there is no reason to suppose they fared better.

'Casualty Return' of 13th Light Dragoons:—

	Men.
Sailed for the West Indies,	452
Died,	287
Drafted to 20th and 21st Light Dragoons,	113
Returned to England,	52
	452

In the 'Digest of Services' of the 14th Hussars,[6] which are kept in the orderly-room at regimental headquarters, the only allusion to this West Indian expedition is as follows:—

> In June 1795 the regiment was dismounted at Clonmel barracks, and marched to Carrick-on-Suir, from whence it embarked to St. Domingo under the command of Colonel Carter. 1797, the regiment, on arrival in England, went to Chelmsford.'

As the above-quoted records are so very meagre, it may be interesting to relate the following facts taken from Cannon's *Historical Record of the 13th Light Dragoons* with reference to the same expedition, in which that regiment also took part:—

> Two troops of the 13th had embarked about July or August 1795 for Jamaica; then the rest of the regiment gave up their horses at Mallow, in Ireland, and sailed from Cork to Bristol. Whilst waiting for orders at Bristol, the 13th Light Dragoons met the 14th Light Dragoons destined for the same service. The Thirteenth subsequently embarked at Southampton in transports; all the ships then laden with troops proceeded from Southampton to Cove Harbour, Cork, and in February 1796 seven troops of the Thirteenth sailed for Barbadoes, where they arrived early in April. The worst revolt had taken place in the island of St. Domingo, which drove a large body of the planters to obtain aid from the English people and to transfer their allegiance from France to the British Crown. In consequence of

---

6. The Regimental Records.

Her Royal Highness Frederica Charlotte Ulrica Catherina
Princess Royal of Prussia, Duchess of York.
Royal Patroness of the Regiment. 26th July 1798.

this, additional forces were ordered to the West Indies.

From Barbadoes the 13th Light Dragoons were moved to St. Domingo; but here the climate was so pestilential, the regiment (which had been supplied with some horses from America) was very soon reduced to a mere skeleton, and lost in six months 20 officers, 7 troop quartermasters, and 233 non-commissioned officers and men, so that the few remaining were removed to Jamaica in December 1796. Here the remnant of the regiment remained until July 1798, and, after transferring some men to the 20th and 21st Light Dragoons, all that remained of the 13th Light Dragoons, 52 souls, embarked for England, and landed at Gravesend in October 1798.

Mr. Peter Vatass, who had been chaplain of the regiment since 24th December 1745, and was now seventy-five years of age, was removed, and no successor seems to have been appointed. Apparently Mr. Vatass had been *on leave* the whole of his service! The salary of a regimental chaplain in those days was about £120 *per annum*.

Major-General Egerton, the new colonel of the Fourteenth, was already well known to them, as he was the staff officer at Clonmel in 1795 when they were ordered to give up their horses after being placed under orders for active service in the West Indies; and when in 1797 they arrived at Chelmsford on return from St. Domingo, he was the Major-General in command there. He always took an intense interest in the regiment, and was extremely proud of the high reputation it subsequently gained in the Peninsula, and he remained at its head till his death in 1823. When he was first appointed to the full Colonelcy he took a very active part in the measures adopted for remounting the regiment and recruiting its diminished ranks after service in the West Indies.

Two 'assistant-surgeons' were for the first time appointed this year, *viz*. Henry Killaly, 1st February 1797; Samuel Newman, 25th April 1797.

1798

The regiment having been recruited and remounted soon mustered 600 sabres: it was divided into 8 troops, and was stationed at Chelmsford. On 26th July 1798 His Majesty King George III. was graciously pleased to approve of the regiment being styled the 14th (or Duchess of York's Own) Regiment of Light Dragoons, in honour of Her Royal Highness the Princess Frederica Charlotte Ulrica Catherina, Princess

Royal of Prussia, who had married H.R.H. the Duke of York in 1791. This honour was conferred for services performed by the 14th Light Dragoons in receiving and escorting H.R.H. the Duchess of York on her arrival in England in the same year. The royal authority was given for the regiment to assume the Prussian Eagle as a badge, and the colour of the facings was changed from lemon-yellow to orange, the colour of the livery of the Royal House of Brandenburg. [7]

The Fourteenth thus lost for a time the original pale yellow colour, but changed from this was revived in 1861 in the colour of the busby-bags when the regiment became Hussars. In the autumn the regiment moved to Braintree and Halstead, where, on 9th October, Major-General Egerton made an inspection. At this review neither the Lieutenant-Colonel (Major-General Grice Blakeney) nor the senior Major (Colonel Arthur Carter) were present, but the junior Major (Lieutenant-Colonel Sir George Dunbar, Bart.) was in command of the regiment. On the 1st January both the Majors were promoted by brevet, Lieutenant-Colonel Carter becoming Colonel, and Major Sir G. Dunbar, Bart., Lieutenant-Colonel.

1799

Being now stationed at Canterbury, the regiment was inspected there on the 25th of September by Major-General Garth. Its establishment was 720, but the effectives on that date were only 450 men and 390 troop-horses.

Major and Brevet-Colonel Arthur Carter, who had practically commanded the regiment for several years, went on 5th December on appointment as Lieutenant-Colonel to the 18th Light Dragoons, and Lieutenant-Colonel John Michel from the unattached list, late 30th Light Dragoons, became second Lieutenant-Colonel of the 14th Light Dragoons on augmentation. Major-General G. Blakeney was still continued as the Lieutenant-Colonel of the regiment though a general officer, and Major (Brevet Lieutenant-Colonel) Sir George Dunbar, Bart.,[8] died on the 15th October.

In the army list for this year a veterinary surgeon appears for the

---

7. Cannon's *Historical Record of the 14th Light Dragoons*. An entry elsewhere gives the date of the royal authority which granted the Prussian Eagle as 7th September 1799. Orange, the colour of the ribbon worn with the Order of the 'Black Eagle,' is still considered the royal colour of Prussia.
8. Dunbar of Mochrum, Wigtonshire
9. The first mention of 'Standing Orders' is in 1784, when Lieutenant-Colonel Blakeney commanded the regiment.

first time in the list of commissioned officers, his name being Samuel Newman, appointed 9th January.

The first paymaster, Mr. James Flanegan, was also appointed this year.

There was an order issued on 22nd April authorising queues ten inches in length to be worn by cavalry and infantry, excepting the light companies.

Captain the Hon. James Butler became major in the regiment.

1800

There were further augmentations in the establishment this year; and there were 3 Lieutenant-Colonels Grice Blakeney, John Michel, and Samuel Hawker, the latter having been appointed on 12th June.

The establishment was raised to 10 troops of 90 rank and file each. Four new guidons were received.

At Canterbury on 1st November the regiment was inspected by Major-General Wilford. A portion of the regiment had lately been in Swinly Camp under Lieutenant-Colonel J. Michel. General Wilford mentions that 'no established orders existed in the corps for its direction and guidance.'

The established code of regimental orders which had existed previously in the regiment, and which was so highly spoken of by the Inspecting General officers from 1784 to 1790, appears to have been allowed to drop out about this period, or perhaps somewhat earlier.

'The system of discipline and good order' established and maintained by the carrying out of these orders is referred to by Major-General Lord Luttrell in his inspection reports of 1785 and 1786, and he gives the credit of it to Colonel Sir John Burgoyne, Bart., who commanded the regiment from 1774 to 1781. His successor in the command, Lieutenant-Colonel Grice Blakeney, who remained at the head of the regiment till he became Lieutenant-General in 1802, appears in the earlier years of his command to have kept up this good regimental system, and adhered to the 'Code of Regimental Orders,' but the latter was allowed to disappear as time went on. [9]

There is no record of the regiment ever having any 'regimental standing orders' again until May 1891, when Colonel H. B. Hamilton at Hounslow introduced the present existing ones, which were then thought to be the first the Fourteenth had ever possessed, as no traces whatever of any previous ones existed, and none apparently had been heard of by anyone living at the time. The reference prov-

ing the former existence of this old 'regimental code of orders' is very interesting, and was discovered by the author of these pages in an old 'Review-Book' of the eighteenth century preserved in the Public Record Office in Chancery Lane, London, where it was deposited by the War Office.

1801

The regiment remained at Canterbury till March. It was at Newbury in April and May. From June it was at Romford and Hornchurch.

On 12th June, Captain Henry Brown became Major, and on 14th August, James Gambier was appointed to the same rank in the regiment. Mr. Robert Thomson became Veterinary Surgeon this year, and remained in that position in the regiment until 10th November 1814.

1802

In consequence of the Peace of Amiens on 27th March 1802, the establishment of the regiment was reduced by two troops.

Captain Neil Talbot became Major on 25th June *vice* J. Gambier, and Lieutenant-Colonel S. Hawker was placed on half-pay owing to the reduction of a Lieutenant-Colonelcy in the establishment of the regiment.

A squadron was stationed under Captain Talbot at Chelmsford during the early part of this year, consisting of 125 troop-horses, and was inspected there on 31st March by Major-General Milner. Lieutenant-Colonel J. Michel became Brevet-Colonel on 29th April, and then succeeded to the command of the Fourteenth, as Major-General Grice Blakeney was promoted Lieutenant-General on the same date, and removed from the regiment after holding the Lieutenant-Colonelcy since 19th November 1781 upwards of 21 years, but it is probable that he had not exercised the active duties of command since his promotion to Major-General on 3rd October 1794. The second Lieutenant-Colonelcy was not filled up. Captain N. Talbot became Major on 25th June.

1803

War broke out again. Considerable augmentations were again ordered, and on the 10th of March the establishment of the regiment was raised to 664 men and 600 troop-horses.

The headquarters were at Hythe in November, where Major-General Cartwright inspected on 5th December.

Colonel J. Michel was succeeded in the Lieutenant-Colonelcy by Lieutenant-Colonel S. Hawker, who was brought back again into the regiment from half-pay to command.

The full Colonel of the regiment, Lieutenant-General John William Egerton, became Earl of Bridgewater.

1804

Further augmentations took place this year, and the regiment now consisted of 10 troops of about 90 rank and file each.

The total gross cost of the regiment for one year came to about £37,857.

The troopers required to complete the regiment up to its augmented establishment were obtained partly by subaltern officers being permitted to raise a stipulated number each for promotion to a higher rank, and partly by the aid of 'recruiting-parties' sent out to various centres. The recruits were chiefly obtained from London, Birmingham, Shrewsbury, and Chichester. In December the establishment was definitely fixed as follows:—

10 Troops.	50 Corporals.
54 Sergeants.	950 Privates.
10 Trumpeters.	1064 Troop-horses.

Captain (Brevet-Major) Richard Pigot became Major on 4th August *vice* H. Browne. Major-General Cartwright inspected the regiment on 1st June at Hythe under command of Lieutenant-Colonel Hawker. The various troops of the Fourteenth were much detached in separate stations same as last year, and had no regular place to assemble in for drill.

Major-General Cartwright made a second inspection in November at the same place (Hythe). In December headquarters were at Guildford, and portions of the regiment at adjacent stations.

1805

In June the regiment moved to Hounslow.

On 22nd August, Major N. Talbot became second Lieutenant-Colonel on augmentation of establishment, and Captain Thomas Smith became Major.

There was a detachment at Kensington under Captain P. Keogh, which consisted of 9 sergeants and 34 corporals, selected from the 10 troops of the regiment.

Whilst stationed at Hounslow, Kensington, Hampton Court, Royal

Escorts, and other adjacent suburban places, the detached troops of the regiment relieved those of the 9th Light Dragoons, and supplied the travelling escorts and letter parties for His Majesty King George in. and other members of the Royal Family, up to the month of September. There were 640 effective troop-horses by the end of the year.

1806

The regiment left Hounslow in July for the south-western district, and headquarters were at Southampton on August 1st, at Winchester August 14th, and at Dorchester on October 14th, having passed through Basingstoke and Alton *en route*.

Captain F. B. Hervey became Major on 8th May *vice* R. Pigot.

1807

In July the regiment left Dorchester, and, after being employed in the early part of the year on election duty in the county of Sussex, for the Midhurst election at Petworth, Fittleworth, and Pullborough, marched *via* Guildford, Farnham, and Bagshot, to its former quarters at Hounslow, Kensington, and Hampton Court.

A supply of new carbines and pistols was issued from the ordnance stores this year to the regiment, including the two augmentation troops, when the whole of the old pistols, carbines, and bayonets were returned into store.

On 9th July, Captain the Honourable Charles Butler became Major *vice* T. Smith.

In September the headquarters of the regiment under Lieutenant-Colonel S. Hawker were at Blatchington, near Brighton, and detachments were stationed at Eastbourne, Hastings, and Bexhill, so the stay at Hounslow must have been very short.

1808

On 5th July the regiment left Blatchington, Eastbourne, Bexhill, and Hastings in four divisions, and marched through London to Ipswich, arriving there 25th July, where it remained three months. On 19th October a depot squadron with heavy baggage was ordered to be left at Ipswich, and the four service squadrons were placed under orders for active service in the Peninsula. The regiment accordingly marched to Tiverton, Taunton, Exeter, and Honiton, one squadron remaining for a time at each place between 16th and 20th November, and on the latter date the four squadrons marched to Flushing, near Falmouth, where they embarked on 5th December on board several transports and sailed for Lisbon. The headquarters were at Romford

on 1st November and at Liskeard on 1st December, previous to embarkation, 5th December.

On 23rd December, under command of Colonel Samuel Hawker, the 14th (Duchess of York's Own) Light Dragoons landed at Lisbon ready to take part in the war against the French.

1809

The French emperor, Napoleon Buonaparte, had already invaded Spain and Portugal, and a British army had proceeded to Portugal to help the Portuguese to expel the invaders. The Portuguese had been successful, and an army under Lieutenant-General Sir John Moore was advancing into Spain, where subsequently, on the 16th January 1809, it was defeated by the French under Marshal Soult, at Corunna, and its gallant leader killed. It was shortly before this catastrophe that the Fourteenth arrived in Portugal to join the British Army, of which Major-General Sir Arthur Wellesley assumed command when he arrived at Lisbon on 22nd April 1809.

Colonel Hawker, commanding the regiment, was appointed A.D.C. to His Majesty King George III. with the rank of Colonel in the army on 25th April. The regiment remained quartered about Lisbon till the spring, when it advanced to Bucellas, an outpost of our army, and formed the advance-guard of the British troops on the march to Coimbra in the month of April. In May the Fourteenth were brigaded with the 16th Light Dragoons and 20th Light Dragoons, as well as with the 3rd Light Dragoons of the King's German Legion, under command of Brigadier-General Stapleton Cotton (afterwards Field-Marshal Viscount Combermere), and took part in a review of the army in Portugal which was held at Coimbra[10] before Lieutenant-General Sir Arthur Wellesley, K.B. (afterwards Field-Marshal the Duke of Wellington); the other cavalry brigade, 3rd and 4th Dragoon Guards, was under the command of Brigadier-General Fane.

The French troops under Marshals Soult and Victor had, in the meantime, invaded Portugal, and Marshal Soult had taken Oporto.[11] The first service undertaken by the British commander was to ex-

---

10. The troops concentrated at Coimbra on 5th May were 25,000 sabres and bayonets, of which 9000 were Portuguese, 3000 Germans, the remainder British. There were also 24 guns. The cavalry division was commanded by Lieutenant-General Payne; the three infantry divisions by Edward Paget (1st), Sherbrooke (2nd), Hill (3rd). Beresford's corps consisted of the Portuguese and a few British troops (Napier.)

11. Cannon's *Historical Record of the 14th Light Dragoons.*

pel the French from the important city of Oporto. Two squadrons of the Fourteenth under Lieutenant-Colonel Neil Talbot were detached with the Portuguese troops under Marshal Beresford to intercept the French if they should attempt to retreat northwards by Amarante. The remaining 3 squadrons under Colonel Hawker advanced direct on Oporto with the main body of the army, when, being employed with the rest of the cavalry on outpost duty and advance-picquets, they had several combats with the enemy, especially on the 10th and 12th May.

It was on the 12th May when Sir Arthur arrived on the banks of the Douro near Oporto, unperceived by the French, who were on the opposite (right) bank. He determined to force a passage across the river, and immediately detached 2 squadrons of the Fourteenth with the German brigade and 2 guns under command of Major-General John Murray 3 miles up the river on the left bank to Barca de Avintas, where they effected a passage in boats. In the meantime Sir Arthur concentrated the main body of his army behind the Serra convent height, where he posted 18 guns in a commanding position on the rock near the convent, and having with difficulty obtained 3 large barges, began to send his troops across.

In his careful observation from the high ground the British general had observed the horses and baggage of the enemy amid clouds of dust retreating along the Vallonga road, and no large force seemed near the river, neither were the guards or patrols vigilant along the banks. There was a large building called the seminary, placed admirably for defence, which also caught the British general's eyes, and large enough to hold two battalions or more. [12]

The first troops to cross were only 25 men under an officer, and these seized and occupied the seminary so quietly that the French in Oporto were not roused. By the time the third boat passed, in which was General Paget, leader of the 1st Division, the city was roused to arms, and the seminary was furiously attacked. General Paget, who had mounted the roof, fell severely wounded, and his place was taken by General Hill, whose division, as well as General Sherbrooke's, were crossing the river in all haste. The English guns from the Serra opposite commanded the enclosure of the seminary and swept the ground on one flank with great effect. The struggle, however, was violent,

---

12. This account of the Douro affair is from Napier's *History of the Peninsular War*, from which numerous extracts have been made and much information gathered and inserted in this *Record*, bearing on this campaign.

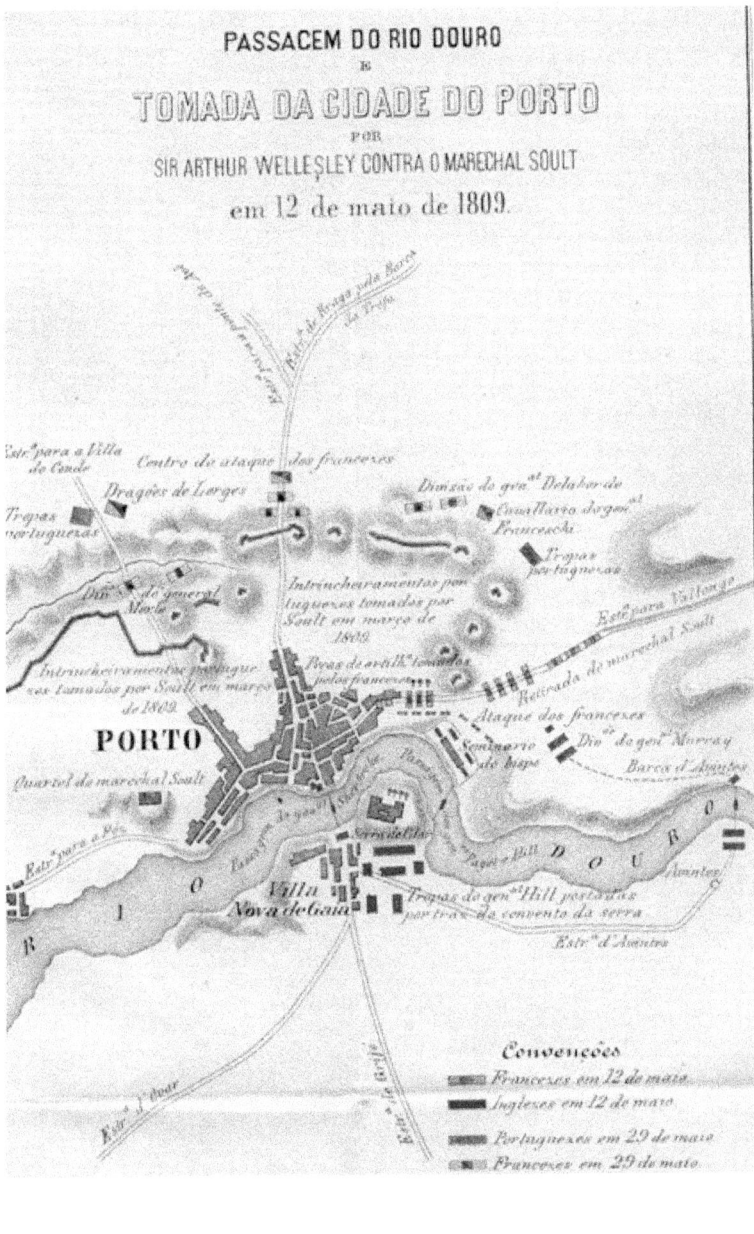

and as the expected help from General Murray did not appear, the position was critical, especially as the numbers of the enemy were so overwhelming.

At length Murray was descried coming down the right bank of the river. About this time the French evacuated the lower city; the attack on the seminary became slacker, and large columns of the enemy were passing in haste and confusion along the Vallonga road. Sherbrooke's men had most opportunely come upon the rear of the French at the lower part of the town, and had taken 5 guns. Murray's arrival across the enemy's line of retreat was of the greatest moment, but as he did not open his guns on the crowds of troops passing along the Vallonga road, Brigadier-General Charles Stewart, just at the right time, headed a most effective charge which was executed by the 2 squadrons of the Fourteenth, one in support of the other, gallantly led by Major F. B. Hervey[13] and Major the Honourable Charles Butler, who charged through the enemy's rear-guard as it was pushing through a narrow road to gain an open space beyond, unhorsed the French general Laborde, and wounded General Foy, but as no support was at hand from Murray's troops, these brave men had to cut their way back with considerable loss. Major Hervey lost his right arm, and the Fourteenth had 12 rank and file killed, 1 rank and file missing. Captain Peter Hawker, Lieutenant Robert Knipe, Lieutenant Evelyn P. Dormer were wounded, as well as 1 sergeant and 18 rank and file.

Napier says:—

> This finished the action. The French continued their retreat; the British remained on the ground they had gained. The latter lost 20 killed, a general and 95 men wounded; the former had 500 men killed and wounded.

The Fourteenth lost heavily, as we have seen, in this affair, but the gallant conduct of the regiment was highly commended in Sir Arthur Wellesley's public despatch as well as in general orders. The troops had marched 85 miles in 4 days over most difficult country, and during 3 of those days they were constantly fighting. The sudden arrival of Murray's Division was a complete surprise to the enemy, and the gallant charge of the 14th Light Dragoons at the critical moment helped in a great measure to turn the tide of victory completely in favour of the British, and to cause the French to make a hasty retreat.

The following is an extract from the general orders issued by Lieu-

---

13. Afterwards Colonel Sir Felton B. Hervey, Bart., C.B., *A.D.C.*

tenant-General Sir Arthur Wellesley, commanding the British forces, dated Oporto, 12th May 1809:—

The passage of the Douro and subsequent movements on the enemy's flank by Lieutenant-General Sherbrooke with the Brigade of Guards and His Majesty's 29th regiment, and the bravery of the two squadrons of the 14th Light Dragoons under command of Major Hervey, and led by Brigadier-General the Honourable Charles Stewart, obtained the victory which has contributed so much to the honour of the troops on this day.

It was not till the year 1837 that permission was given for the regiment to bear the word 'Douro' on its appointments.

The 14th Light Dragoons were now employed with the separate corps under Marshal Beresford in following up the French army under Marshal Soult as far as Ginjo. Here they halted, and afterwards moved to Abrantes on the Tagus, where the British Army was concentrated for further operations. On 27th June an advance was made in the direction of Talavera de la Reyna, through Castello Brancho, Placentia, and the valley of the Alberche in Estremadura. On 15th July the British headquarters were at Placentia.

According to Napier, Sir Arthur Wellesley had now about 21,000 men with 30 guns, and Cuesta's Spaniards numbered about 35,000 with 70 guns.

The British had one cavalry division, 6 regiments, 3047 sabres, under Lieutenant-General Payne in three brigades; 3rd and 4th Dragoon Guards under Fane, 14th and 16th Light Dragoons under Cotton, and the cavalry of the King's German Legion under Anson.

Four divisions of infantry as follows:—

1st, Lieutenant-General Sherbroke;
2nd, Major-General Hill;
3rd, Major-General Mackenzie;
4th, Brigadier-General Campbell.

The artillery was commanded by Major-General Howarth.

On the march through Spain the British army suffered great privations from scarcity of provisions; and the incapacity of the Spanish general, as well as the unreliable nature of his troops, caused Sir Arthur much anxiety, and greatly hampered his movements. Towards the end of July two of the British divisions were sent forward, as well as the whole of the cavalry, to support a movement of the Spaniards against

Marshal Victor's army, which, according to reports circulated, was falling back on Torrijos and behind the Guadarama River. Lieutenant-Generals Sherbrooke and Payne commanded this force.

On the 26th July the Spanish Army under Cuesta was at St. Ollalla, Sherbrooke was at Cassalegas, Sir Arthur Wellesley was at Talavera, and Marshal Victor's army was only a few miles from Cuesta's advanced posts with 50,000 men and 90 guns. The French had also an army of 50,000 men under Mortier at Salamanca. The Spaniards were driven back by Victor, and had to retire on Talavera, supported by Sherbrooke and the cavalry under Payne.

On the 27th July a battle was imminent, and Sir Arthur left Mackenzie's Division with a brigade of cavalry to cover a retrograde movement, whilst he withdrew the allies into a position for order of battle six miles in rear. General Mackenzie was left in a wood lying to the right of the Alberche, which covered his left flank. Between 2 and 3 o'clock this post was attacked by the French, when the 14th Light Dragoons were ordered to advance, and they crossed the River Alberche, sending out a line of skirmishers to cover the retirement of the infantry. The regiment was kept out skirmishing till nightfall, and lost 9 horses killed; one officer, Lieutenant Theophilus T. Ellis, and one private soldier being wounded, and two horses missing. [14]

After performing this service the Fourteenth resumed the post assigned them in the allied army, which was in the rear of Brigadier-General Campbell's Division. The position was as follows: the Spaniards were placed on the right of our line, their right resting on Talavera; on their left came Campbell's Division, in two lines; Sherbrooke's Division came next to Campbell's, in one line only; Mackenzie's Division was destined to be the second line to Sherbrooke's; Hill's Division was to be on the left of the line. The whole line was two miles long, and was an exceedingly well chosen and strong position. The British and Germans mustered about 20,000 men under arms, with 30 guns. The Spaniards had about 34,000 men and 70 guns. The French numbered 80 guns and 50,000 men, and they were hardy veterans, while the allies had only 19,000 genuine soldiers. [15] King Joseph Buonaparte was in command, with Jourdan, Victor, and many other renowned generals under him.

At daybreak on the morning of the 28th July, the British left was attacked by the enemy's artillery and infantry, then the centre, lastly

---

14. This was the combat of Salinas mentioned by Napier.
15. Napier.

the right of the line became involved in fierce contest. Both sides suffered heavily, the enemy more. At last the French retired in disorder to their original position, still keeping up a powerful fire of artillery.[16]

Our artillery was no match for the French: it was small of calibre and the guns few in number. When Cuesta was asked for reinforcements he sent two guns, but luckily these were good and well served by the Spaniards. Sir Arthur now sent for his cavalry, which was at a considerable distance; he also obtained some Spanish cavalry, and placed the whole in mass six lines deep, the leading squadrons looking down a valley on his left flank. After this, about 9 o'clock, there was a cessation of hostilities for several hours.[17]

It was not till 12 o'clock that further hostilities took place. Then the French opened the fight with 80 pieces of cannon, followed by the advance of their light troops, who were supported by broad black columns in rear. Campbell's Division was first attacked with fury, but it stood firm; Mackenzie's Brigade and his Spanish battalions gallantly with-stood the onslaught, and after repulsing a second attack no less vehement, aided by a flank charge of Spanish cavalry, secured the victory in that quarter. On our left, a brilliant charge of Anson's Brigade of cavalry took place, when the 23rd Light Dragoons under Colonel Seymour and Major F. Ponsonby, with the 1st German Hussars under Colonel Arentschild, charged Villate's troops.

In this charge Colonel Arentschild, seeing an impracticable piece of ground ahead of him, pulled up his regiment just in time to avoid a catastrophe; but the 23rd Light Dragoons, continuing their advance, got into difficulties, and still going forward, were at last completely overmatched by the enemy. They then had to retire, leaving half their numbers killed and wounded considerably more than 200.[18]

The British centre was very hard pressed by Lapisse's attack, and here it was that Sherbrooke's men bravely drove back their assailants, when, encouraged by success, the Guards and Germans incautiously made a bayonet charge, in which the pursuit was carried too far, until our men were finally repulsed by the French reserves of infantry and dragoons. Confusion ensued, which caused the centre of the line to give way and become hopelessly broken: our right and left flanks, however, remained firm and resolute, Campbell and Hill holding their positions against all attacks. Sir Arthur saw that a critical and perilous moment had come, and was determined to make a final effort to restore the centre.

16, 17 & 18. Napier.

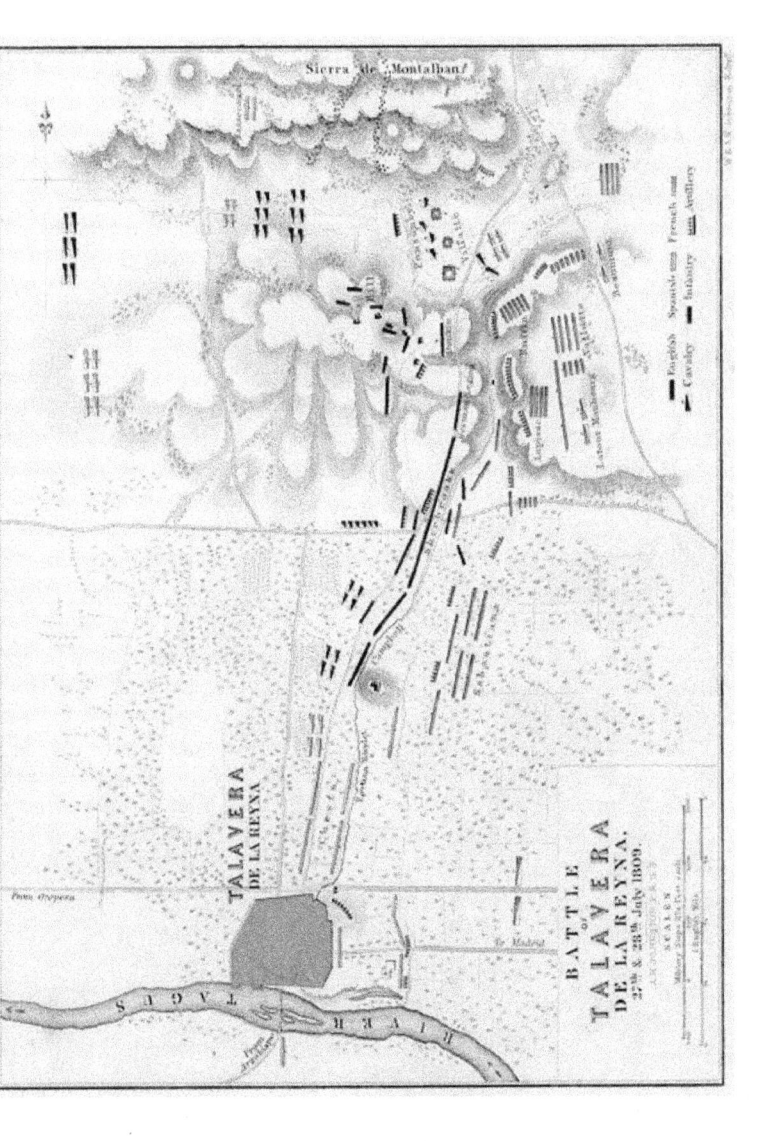

Suddenly the 48th Regiment, led by Colonel Donellan, was seen advancing from the hill right down on the flank of the victorious French columns, pouring in such a steady and destructive fire of musketry as completely checked the enemy's further movements. This enabled the Guards and Germans to rally, whilst our guns played incessantly on their opponents, and to crown all, a brigade of light cavalry under Brigadier-General Cotton, consisting of the 14th and 16th Light Dragoons, was seen rapidly advancing on the enemy's flank. This cavalry attack brought matters to a crisis: the enemy was checked, began to waver, lost all impulse, the battle was won. [19]

A general retirement to their former position subsequently took place along the French line. The British were too exhausted by fatigue and weakened by losses to attempt any pursuit, and no assistance could be given by the Spaniards. At 6 o'clock all fighting ceased, and both armies remained on their own positions. Thus it was that the 14th Light Dragoons, 16th Light Dragoons, and the 48th Regiment, by coming forward at the critical time when the Guards Brigade was almost annihilated, contributed in no small measure to change the fortunes of the day, and to gain the victory for the British arms.

The Fourteenth lost at Talavera:—
   Killed—21 horses, 3 men.
   Wounded—5 officers—
      Colonel S. Hawker, slightly.
      Captain J. Chapman, Captain P. Hawker,
         Lieutenant W. Wainman and Lieutenant
         Thomas Smith severely.
   ,,   6 men.
   ,,   3 horses.
   Missing— 13 horses.
   Taken prisoner—Lieutenant E. P. Dormer.
Lieutenant-Colonel Talbot and Captain Baker had horses killed under them in this battle.
The total losses of the British at Talavera were—
   Killed—33 officers, including Generals Mackenzie
      and Langworth, 800 men.
   Wounded—195 officers, including 3 generals, 3700 men.
   Missing—9 officers, 650 men.
In addition there were about 800 killed and wounded on the 27th, the day before the battle.

---
19. Napier.

The Spaniards lost 1200 men.
The French lost 7389 officers and men.

Colonel Hawker was rewarded with a gold medal, and the Fourteenth subsequently (1820) received authority to bear on the guidons and appointments the word 'Talavera,' in commemoration of their distinguished services in this action. [20]

After the victory of Talavera, the French brought forward such overwhelming armies in different directions under Ney, Soult, Victor, Mortier, and other generals, with the intention of cutting off and utterly crushing the allies, that Sir Arthur Wellesley decided to act for some time on the defensive, and withdrew his army towards Truxillo and Merida, moving along the left bank of the Tagus, so as to baffle, if he could, the strong combination of armies against him. At first he moved to Deleytoza, crossing the river at Arzobispo, Craufurd's Brigade and six guns being sent to secure the boat-bridge at Almaraz and to cut off the French.

About the end of August, owing to various circumstances, principally the scarcity of supplies and the bad conduct of the Spanish army, Sir Arthur fell back into Portugal, and occupied the valley of the Guadiana, his troops being distributed in Badajos, Elvas, Campo Major, etc., but the men suffered considerably from malignant fever in these districts. The Fourteenth were removed to Villa Viçosa, a town in Alemtejo (Portugal), and in December they moved to Santarem, situated on the right bank of the Tagus, in the Estremadura of Portugal. Here they were formed in brigade under Major-General Slade with the 1st Royal Dragoons, a regiment recently come from England.

During this year the rank of Troop-Sergeant-Major was introduced into the cavalry. The establishment of officers in the regiment at this time was—

1 Colonel.	1 Adjutant (included in Lieutenants).
2 Lieutenant-Colonels.	2 Majors.
1 Surgeon.	9 Captains.
1 Assistant Surgeon.	21 Lieutenants.
1 Veterinary Surgeon.	8 Cornets.
1 Quartermaster,	1 Paymaster.

The regimental agents were Messrs. Collyer and Son, London.

Quartermasters became commissioned officers about this year. The

---

20. Cannon.

first commissioned quartermaster in the Fourteenth was Mr. Jameson, appointed 4th January 1810.

1810

The 14th Light Dragoons had a regimental song [21] at this period, as follows:—

OLD REGIMENTAL SONG OF 14TH LIGHT DRAGOONS,
Used in the Peninsular War.

'*Ça Ira!*' [22] 1810

Beaten backward in the press
Reeled the Old Fourteenth,
And in triumph shrill arose
The yell of the triumphant foes,
As, where the British Lion flew,
Flaunting 'White and Red and Blue
Full well the fiery Frenchmen knew
The fame of the Fourteenth.

Beaten backward in the press
Reeled the Old Fourteenth,
Cheerily their Colonel spoke
As the red line round him broke,
Laughing, waving with his hand
To the leader of the band,
As again they took their stand,
The men of the Fourteenth.

'Play the Frenchman's March,' he said,
The chief of the Fourteenth;
'Strike it up, strike loud and clear,
As 1 stand before you here,
We will prove our mettle soon,
Ere yon pale sun rides at noon,
We'll beat them to their own brave tune,
We men of the Fourteenth.'

On 14th March the Fourteenth left Santarem and returned to the Alemtejo and took the advanced posts of Lieutenant-General Rowland Hill's Corps at Arronches, a town situate at the conflux of the

---

21. This song was kindly presented by Mr. F. A. Hawker, son of the late General Sir S. Hawker, G.C.H. Mr. Hawker also kindly gave the photograph of his father which is reproduced in this *Record*.
22. '*Ça ira!*' (French) = 'We shall succeed.'

Caya and the Aigrette, near the Spanish confines. In June the Fourteenth advanced to Almeida in the Beira province, and were attached to the Light Division under Brigadier-General Craufurd, who was behind the Agueda River watching the enemy's movements, when, with the 16th Light Dragoons and 1st Hussars (King's German Legion), they took the outpost duty on this frontier.

Ciudad Rodrigo was at this time being invested by Marshal Ney. Marauding parties of French used to enter the villages of Barquilla and Villa de Puerco; ambuscades were formed to cut them off: the Fourteenth took part in them. On 11th July a portion of the regiment charged a square of French infantry 200 strong: the square withstood the charge and opened a terrific fire. The gallant Lieutenant-Colonel Talbot, Quartermaster M'Cormick, and 11 men were killed close up to the bayonets, and 23 men were wounded. This occurred near Sexmiro, in front of Ciudad Rodrigo, and as Colonel Hawker had gone home wounded after Talavera, Lieutenant-Colonel Talbot was virtually in command of the regiment at the time of his death.

Major F. B. Hervey succeeded him as second Lieutenant-Colonel on 2nd August, and he assumed command of the regiment in the absence of Colonel Hawker, immediately after Lieutenant-Colonel Talbot fell, and subsequently when Colonel Hawker was appointed Major-General in 1811, he became the real commanding officer of the regiment, and it was under his able leadership that the 14th Light Dragoons became famous as Light Cavalry, being specially celebrated for the excellent manner in which they performed their outpost duties. Captain J. Chapman was promoted Major on the same date, in succession to Lieutenant-Colonel Hervey.

Captain Brotherton, late of the 14th Light Dragoons (afterwards General Sir T. W. Brotherton, G.C. B., who died in 1868), has left a graphic account of the death and burial of Lieutenant-Colonel Talbot, amongst other interesting incidents [23] of his experiences in the Peninsula when serving in the Fourteenth, as follows:—

> The most formidable thing for cavalry to deal with is a square of steady infantry indeed, such a square may be said to bid defiance to cavalry unless the cavalry has the aid of artillery to batter the square before charging it; for the formation, in square, to resist cavalry is a most murderous one when exposed to artillery.

---

23. These incidents are in MSS., and were kindly presented by the late Colonel the Hon. G. H. Gough, C.B.

At the village of Sexmiro we encountered a square of French infantry. It was lying down, concealed in some high-standing corn, and only rose up when my squadron came within pistol-shot of it, and was beautifully steady. We charged it most gallantly, but they fired a deadly volley into us, and half my men fell killed or wounded. Colonel Talbot, who commanded the regiment, had put himself at the head of the squadron along with me. Poor fellow, he fell pierced by eight balls, literally on the enemy's bayonets. The moment the square had fired into and so sadly crippled us, it moved off to join its support close by, and we were so shattered as not to be able to follow.

The French infantry behaved beautifully on this occasion. It was the 61st of the line. Marshal Massena immediately bestowed the Cross of the Legion of Honour on the officer commanding and several of the non-commissioned officers and men. So steady and cool was this little square, that though my horse fell, with the wounded, within two yards of their ranks, not a man moved out to bayonet me, but the square immediately retired in admirable order. We were repulsed, suffered great loss, and left our commanding officer, amongst others, dead on the field. I was sent afterwards to ask for his body, and brought it in. It was taken into a tent in which we messed.

We all felt deep grief at his loss, for we all loved him; yet I never shall forget that we ate a hearty meal with our beloved friend's corpse close to us, uncovered. He had a glorious countenance in death. He was a noble-looking fellow, and had died so instantaneously, having had no less than eight balls through him, that his countenance was but little altered. We buried him on the glacis of Fort Conception, and a few days after I saw his body blown into the air, along with the fragments of the fort, when the explosion took place.

What became of his remains afterwards we never could ascertain, as several horses and men were killed at the same time by the explosion. I may add that I went out with a flag of truce to fetch his body. When I arrived at the fatal spot where the murderous charge of my squadron had taken place, I saw lying on the ground only three French soldiers, one of whom was dead and the other two much mutilated by our sabres, but this was all the execution we had done in return for our severe loss. I brought poor Talbot's body back, and we buried him (as already related) on the glacis of Fort Conception. A few days afterwards the premeditated explosion of this fort took place, when his body was blown into the air. The blowing up and complete destruction of this important and beautiful little Star Fort which guarded the frontier of Spain, was an operation of extreme delicacy, and of most critical and precarious execution, for Colonel Burgoyne,[24] the talented officer of Engineers, selected for the task, had positive orders not to blow it up till the very last moment (that is, till the advance of the enemy), so that we might make use of it till the last moment, but not leave a vestige of it for the enemy's use.

These instructions were carried into effect with extraordinary precision and most thoroughly, though Massena had the meanness and effrontery to say the contrary in his report to Napoleon. I had some little share in the execution of this critical operation. I happened to be on picquet in front of the fort on the night it took place, or rather the morning, at daybreak. As it was a matter of great importance to Massena to preserve the fort, if possible, and prevent its destruction, which he knew was planned, he thought he would best obtain this object by a sudden and rapid advance on our picquets, driving them back at a gallop, and arriving on the glacis of the fort as soon as we did, when, he thought, the officer of engineers would hesitate to blow it up for fear of destroying our people. The match was always kept ready in the fort for instantaneous explosion.

Knowing the state of the case, I had only just time to exclaim to an officer close to me (named Wainman), who was beautifully mounted on a thoroughbred horse, to go at speed to Burgoyne and apprise him that we were being driven back most rapidly, and that we had no time to lose. He arrived at the fort only just in time to enable Burgoyne to explode the mine. I found myself on the glacis just at this moment, and lost several horses and men by the explosion, besides the harrowing sight of poor Talbot's body being blown into the air. I had brought the body slung across a troop-horse. He was a delightful fellow, a friend I most deeply regretted, but singular and eccentric, particularly in his dress. He was dressed, the day he was killed, in nankeen pantaloons. Never was anything like the grief for his loss. When we buried him not an eye was dry.

---

24. Afterwards Field-Marshal Sir John Burgoyne, Bart., G.C.B.

Napier says that four squadrons of the Fourteenth, under Lieutenant-Colonel Talbot, took part in this charge against the French infantry square.

On 11th July, Ciudad Rodrigo surrendered, the Fourteenth remained in the villages near Fort La Conception until the 21st July, when, as the French were approaching in masses, they fell back to Almeida. Here Brigadier-General Craufurd was bold enough to halt and make a stand against the advancing enemy, which led to the combat of Coa, in which the Light Division suffered heavily, and lost over 300 men.

Early in the morning of the 24th July, after a wet and stormy night on outpost duty, a skirmishing right took place with the French troops, who were advancing in force, near the passage of the River Coa, when the Light Division was engaged for a considerable time against superior numbers of the vanguard of the French Army commanded by Marshal Massena.

On this occasion the Fourteenth were engaged and had the following casualties: killed—1 sergeant; wounded—Lieutenant Blatchford, 1 man and 4 horses.

Brigadier-General Craufurd stated in his despatch:—

The retirement of the 14th Light Dragoons from Val-de-la-mula to Almeida was carried out in the most regular and soldier-like manner, though opposed to a superior force of French cavalry.

Lord Wellington's headquarters were now at Alverca.

General Brotherton relates the following as to the fight at Coa:—

The combat of the Coa took place on 24th July 1810, and was a very sharp affair; where we were only 6000 strong, against 24,000 brought into action by Massena. There were many gallant and daring deeds done that day, in taking and re-taking the bridge over the river of the same name. In one of these attacks, one of the officers of the 43rd, (Frederick) brother of Sir Richard —— of Barwood Park, was shot through the leg. Happening to be close to him, I jumped off my horse to assist him. He was bleeding profusely, and no surgeon immediately at hand to stop it, I had my canteen slung round me full of strong wine, and put it to his mouth, and made him take a copious draught of it.

Just as I had done this the surgeon of the regiment came up, and I told him what I had done, at which he expressed himself displeased, saying that probably I should be the cause of his death; but he (Frederick ———) always said afterwards to everybody that I had saved his life by giving him the wine, as he felt so faint that he felt he was dying. He lived afterwards in excellent health till the 21st June 1854.

On the same day (24th July 1810) one of the officers under my immediate command, Cornet B———, was hit by a fragment of a shell in the posterior, and as he was rather a soft sort of fellow, I thought, at first, that he made too great a fuss about it, though he turned deadly pale. But he had good reason to complain, for the piece of shell had buried itself deep in his buttock, and caused his death.

From Almeida to the lines of Torres Vedras the regiment in conjunction with the 16th Light Dragoons and 1st Hussars, King's German Legion, under the command of Lieutenant-General Sir S. Cotton, Bart.,[25] formed the rear-guard of the army.

On 28th August one squadron, acting with a squadron of the 1st Royal Dragoons at Frexadas, was engaged with a superior force of the enemy and highly distinguished itself.

The advanced posts of the British army having removed to Frexadas, the French besieged and took Almeida on the 20th August, and on the day following they attacked a squadron of the Royals and one of the 14th Light Dragoons on picquet at Frexadas, under Major Dorville of the Royals. The enemy brought forward a superior force of cavalry supported by infantry, but the two squadrons, undaunted by the greater numbers, charged the French with signal gallantry and drove them from the field with the loss of many men killed and wounded and 8 prisoners. The Royals lost 2 men and 1 horse wounded.[26]

On 24th September, when the enemy skirmished with our picquets near Mortagao, a squadron of the 14th Light Dragoons under Captain T. W. Brotherton, acting with a squadron of 16th Light Dragoons and a squadron of 1st King's German Hussars, covered the retreat of the Light Division for 4 miles. These 3 squadrons drove back 4 squadrons of French Hussars, and the squadron of the Fourteenth charged the enemy's cavalry, killing 30 men.

On 25th September, Captain the Honourable H. Percy was taken

---
25. Afterwards Field-Marshal Viscount Combermere, G.C.B., G.C.H.
26. General De Ainslie's *Royal Dragoons, 1887.*

prisoner whilst reconnoitring near the heights of Busaco. On this occasion the regiment, together with the Royals, was employed to cover the retreat of the Light Division to the position of Busaco. Whilst performing this duty against the masses of the French Army advancing on Busaco during the 25th and 26th September, the casualties of the 14th Light Dragoons were as follows:—

Killed—1 horse.
Wounded—1 sergeant, 2 rank and file, 4 horses.
Missing—3 rank and file, 7 horses.

The Fourteenth were now in brigade with the 1st Royal Dragoons under Major-General Slade, and Lieutenant-General Sir Stapleton Cotton commanded the Cavalry Division.

On the 27th September, at the Battle of Busaco, the Fourteenth, together with the 1st Royal Dragoons, were in reserve. Subsequently they were employed in covering the retreat of the army to the strong lines of Torres Vedras. This important battle, after hard fighting, resulted in a victory for the allies. The French lost 800 killed and 1 general, Grain-d'Orge, with a total loss of about 4500, whilst the allies only lost 1300. The position taken up by Lord Wellington was impregnable, and Marshal Massena, after his repulse, marched towards Coimbra, whilst the Allies crossed the Mondego near Coimbra, and moved towards Condeixa and Pombal.

General Brotherton relates the following incidents about Busaco:—

At the Battle of Busaco, after the charge made on our position by General Simon was repulsed, several of the French soldiers, who had fallen wounded within a few yards of our line, lay gasping in agony and thirst, calling out for water to drink; but such was the galling fire still kept up by the enemy on this point, that it appeared almost certain death for any one to show himself for an instant beyond the shelter which some rocks afforded. I observed, however, a noble young fellow, a Hanoverian belonging to the German Legion, walk coolly and deliberately from behind a rock, and going to the nearest wounded French soldier who was calling out for drink, but lay in a most contorted and painful position (one of his legs, which was broken by a musket-shot, being bent under him), applied his canteen to the poor fellow's mouth, after having, without the least degree of hurry or trepidation (though the fire continued most heavy), settled his head on his knapsack, and otherwise made his position less painful. The fine young fellow did this successively to several other wounded Frenchmen, and then returned to his regiment.

When first this young officer stepped out, the enemy, fancying he might be leading an attack, redoubled their fire, but when they perceived what he was doing, the firing immediately ceased, and was succeeded by vociferous cheering at his conduct. A more affecting scene I never beheld in the field, and I only regret that, almost at the same moment, I witnessed a disgusting contrast to it. A staff officer, a German, whose name I shall abstain from mentioning, placed himself in perfect security behind a rock, and with a rifle, with which he piqued himself on being an unerring shot, kept picking off French officers and soldiers by way of amusement! I remonstrated with him on his barbarous conduct, and shamed him out of it, but not before he had hit several poor fellows who were actually employed at the time in burying their dead (it was a working-party sent out for the purpose). The remembrance of such conduct makes my blood curdle in my veins even at this time.

At this same battle (Busaco) I witnessed an instance of the nervousness and superstition of the bravest soldiers. A battalion of the German Legion (Hanoverians) was sent down to drive the French out of a wood which they occupied in our front. They drove the enemy out most gallantly, but immediately after came running back most wildly and unaccountably till we learnt the cause. It appeared that part of the enemy's troops occupying the wood were part of the German contingent in the French service, and amongst them were some Hanoverians. On finding this out, our Hanoverians fled with the utmost precipitation out of the wood they had so gallantly gained possession of, horrified at the idea of fighting against their countrymen, and perhaps their relatives.

Another of the general's stories is well worth relating. He says:—

On the retreat of the army to the famous lines of Torres Vedras, when in command of the rearguards, a whole convent of nuns came running out of their convent, as I passed by it, and implored me to save them from the French. It was impossible for me to stop to protect them, and yet I could not bring myself to leave the poor creatures to the tender mercies of the French soldiers, though they were neither young nor handsome, but old and sallow, from penance and vigils, no doubt; so I resolved on the expedient of placing these poor distracted creatures (22 in number) *en croupe* behind as many dragoons. They had uneasy seats, but clasped the dragoons tightly round their waists, and we brought them safe into the lines of Torres Vedras, to their great joy and to the great amusement of all those who saw my convoy such an one as had never before, I suppose, been escorted in this manner by dragoons. Lord Wellington heard of this adventure, and was much amused by it, and the next time I dined with him, after it took place, he complimented me on my chivalrous affair and laughed heartily about it.

I was not so fortunate with a cargo of a very different description which I once attempted also to carry off *en croupe*. It was a famous "Murillo" altar-piece at Medina de Ris Secco, in Castile. One of the priests came running out to me as I was patrolling through the streets in search of the enemy, and told me of this famous picture, and advised me, as the French were momentarily expected, to have it taken down, rolled up, and placed carefully between two dragoons, the ends resting on their valises, for it was a large picture.

Ill-luck, however, would have it that the French never entered Medina at this period, and knowing how I should get blamed for taking away this picture except to save it from the French, I was obliged, after having carried it a considerable distance, to retrace my steps, having heard of the retreat of the enemy, and replace the picture whence I had taken it. It was afterwards, however, taken away by Marshal Soult, and is, I believe, at this moment part of his dishonestly acquired collection. He was one of the most unscrupulous plunderers in the French Army, and this is saying a great deal for him!

All this time the French legions in overwhelming numbers were still pressing on, and the 14th Light Dragoons formed the rearguard of our army as far as Pombal. On the 1st of October Lord Wellington's outposts were drawn in from the heights of Coimbra, on which occasion 3 troops of the Fourteenth under Major the Honourable Charles Butler constituted the rearguard, and they proceeded through the town in rear of the Light Division, and then acted on the main road leading to Pombal. The remainder of the regiment was acting on the plain with the rest of the cavalry of the army, but had to withdraw before the superior force of the enemy, crossing the Mondego at a ford below the town, and then skirmishing to prevent the passage of that river by the French. Here some sharp fighting took place, and the enemy's cavalry attacked and cut down some of the British in the middle of the river, and altogether 50 or 60 men were lost.

That night (1st October) the British headquarters were at Redinha, having passed through Condeixa, eight miles from Coimbra, and next day they were at Leiria. The retreat now became somewhat hasty and disordered, and plundering commenced, but Lord Wellington took vigorous measures to enforce discipline. At Leiria, three men taken in the act were hanged. On the evening of the 4th October the French drove the English picquets from Pombal, and next morning came so suddenly upon Leiria as to create general confusion. There were daily encounters going on between our rearguard and the enemy's advanced bodies, and the Fourteenth had frequent opportunities of proving their valour, which they certainly did not fail to take advantage of.

At Rio Mandevilla, together with the 1st Royal Dragoons, the 16th Light Dragoons, the 1st German Hussars, and Captain Bull's troop of artillery, they repulsed a very superior force, on which occasion the 1st French Hussars were nearly annihilated. The English lost 3 officers and 50 men, and the French many more: it is believed the enemy had 36 squadrons opposed to 10. The casualties of the Fourteenth at Rio Mandevilla were—6 men killed; 8 men, 12 horses wounded, and also on 4th, 5th, 8th, and 9th October they lost 1 man wounded, and 12 men and 2 horses missing.

On the 10th, Lord Wellington occupied the fortified lines of Torres Vedras, where the Fourteenth took charge of the outposts on the line from the Sobral road in front of Torres Vedras so long as the French Army under Marshal Massena, Prince of Essling, remained opposed to us in the vicinity of these stupendous lines of defensive works. Here the two armies watched one another for a considerable time, but at length, after frequent reconnoitring, the French commanders declined to attack, and during the night of the 14th November, Massena retired and established his army upon the heights of Santarem, where he remained till the night of the 5th March 1811.

The morning of the 15th November was foggy, and the retreat of the enemy was not discovered for several hours after daybreak. The

Fourteenth were ordered forward along the Cartaxo road, and their advanced patrols took a number of stragglers prisoners. The British headquarters were soon re-established at Cartaxo, where the regiment was entrusted with the outposts extending from the causeway and bridge over the river.

Captain Brotherton relates the following incident with reference to the affair at Sobral:—

> On the last day of our retreat into the famous lines of Torres Vedras before Massena's army, we had a very sharp affair at a place called Sobral, so much so that we were hotly engaged and literally intermixed with the enemy, particularly the 71st Foot, the Rifles, and ourselves, the 14th Light Dragoons. The enemy were in very superior force, and we were giving way very fast. At this moment Colonel (then Captain) Perceval fell close to me, pierced by two balls, one through his leg and another through his arm. He was on the point of falling into the hands of the enemy. In those days I was particularly active, and as we were running away, I could use my legs as well as anybody, so I dismounted, and put poor Perceval on my horse, and joined in the scramble on foot, till I came up to a mounted dragoon of my own regiment.
>
> As, in action, the presence and exertions of an officer are more valuable than those of a private, it is not only justifiable, but it is incumbent on an officer, sooner than leave the field, to dismount a private, and take his horse. This I accordingly did without having time to ask any questions. When the fight was over, the late General Sir Denis Packe, a warm-hearted but very passionate man, whose orderly I had unknowingly dismounted, came up to me and lectured me most severely and harshly for having done so; and certainly, had I known the man was orderly to a general officer, I would not have dismounted him, as it is essential for a general to have his orderly in action. I had presence of mind enough to make no reply, but bear the reprimand in silence.
>
> The general went away, but his *aide-de-camp*, Captain Synge (now Colonel Synge), having informed him of the circumstances under which I had taken his orderly's horse, he returned and made me many apologies for having reprimanded me, and praised what I had done. It was a heartfelt satisfaction to have

saved poor Perceval, who, to the last day of his life, was grateful for it. He died at Brussels in 1838, and his wife has told me since that almost with his last breath he exclaimed, "*Generous Brotherton; he once saved my life!*" This was very gratifying to me.

On 20th October a trumpet-major was authorised to be borne on the establishment of cavalry regiments with the pay a of a sergeant. Cavalry regiments of ten troops to have one trumpet-major and nine trumpeters.

The following: is one of General Brotherton's anecdotes of what occurred when the Fourteenth were at Torres Vedras:—

When we were in the famous lines of Torres Vedras, I had gone to dinner, to some friends of the Guards, on a mule, and returning to my regimental bivouac at night, I became apprehensive of going into an enemy's picquet by mistake. I came to a turning which I thought I knew well, and tried to turn my mule to the *left*, which I thought was the right road, but he insisted on going to the *right*. We had a great battle, but all I could do was in vain, and he carried me his own way, to the *right*, and I got safe to my camp. I had the curiosity next morning to go to the spot where the mule and myself had differed in opinion, when I found that he was not only right, but that I was so wrong, that, if I had had my own way, I should have gone right into the enemy's camp.

1811

In the Army List for this year the regiment appears with—

1 Colonel.	1 Paymaster.
2 Lieutenant-Colonels.	1 Veterinary Surgeon.
2 Majors.	1 Adjutant.
10 Captains.	1 Surgeon.
22 Lieutenants.	2 Assistant-Surgeons.
7 Cornets.	1 Quartermaster.

Agents—Messrs. Collyer, London.

On the 15th February, Viscount Wellington's headquarters were at Cartaxo. The Fourteenth were still in brigade with the 1st Royal Dragoons, and their brigadier was Major-General Slade.

On 6th March, at daybreak, Viscount Wellington discovered that the French had retreated and left their camp at Santarem. Marshal Massena was really forced to take this step, his army having become so wasted by sickness and privation. Our troops accordingly advanced in pursuit, the Fourteenth still being employed on outpost duty, and forming part of the advance-guard of the army.

On 8th March, Captain Babington's squadron, supported by the remainder of the regiment under Lieutenant-Colonel Hervey, made a brilliant and most successful charge against four squadrons of the 11th and 26th French Dragoons at Venta de Serra, capturing 14 men and 14 horses, and losing only 2 men and 2 horses.

The regiment was now engaged in the different skirmishes and actions which were fought by our troops against the rear of the retreating enemy, the principal of which were:—

Pombal,	10th March.
Redinha,	12th March.
Casal Nova,	14th March.
Foz D'Aronce,	15th March.
Battle of Sabugal,	3rd April.
Miranda de Colvo.	
Tay D'Aortos.	

In these various engagements in which the Fourteenth took part, they escaped without any casualties.

The French Army were heavy losers in the fight at Sabugal, where they were unskilfully handled by Reynier, and lost 1500 men to the allies' 200. Wellington said, 'This was one of the most glorious actions British troops were ever engaged in.' The whole affair did not last an hour. It took place on the banks of the Coa: Reynier had to attack the British uphill. The 43rd and 52nd Regiments of Light Infantry particularly distinguished themselves under Brigadier-General Beckwith, and captured a howitzer. Brigadier-General Colville's Brigade of the 3rd Division by a resolute fire on the French left decided the victory, and our cavalry pursued the flying enemy in their retreat to Rendo and Alfayates. The larger portion of the French army had reached Ciudad Rodrigo about the 4th April, and from thence Marshal Massena, Prince of Essling, continued his retrograde movement to Salamanca, which he occupied.

Wellington was now on the confines of Portugal, and invested Almeida. The Light Division occupied Gallegos and Espeja, whilst the rest of his army was disposed in villages on both sides of the Coa, and the headquarters were settled at Villa Formosa on the frontiers of Spain and Portugal. The Fourteenth furnished the outposts on the left

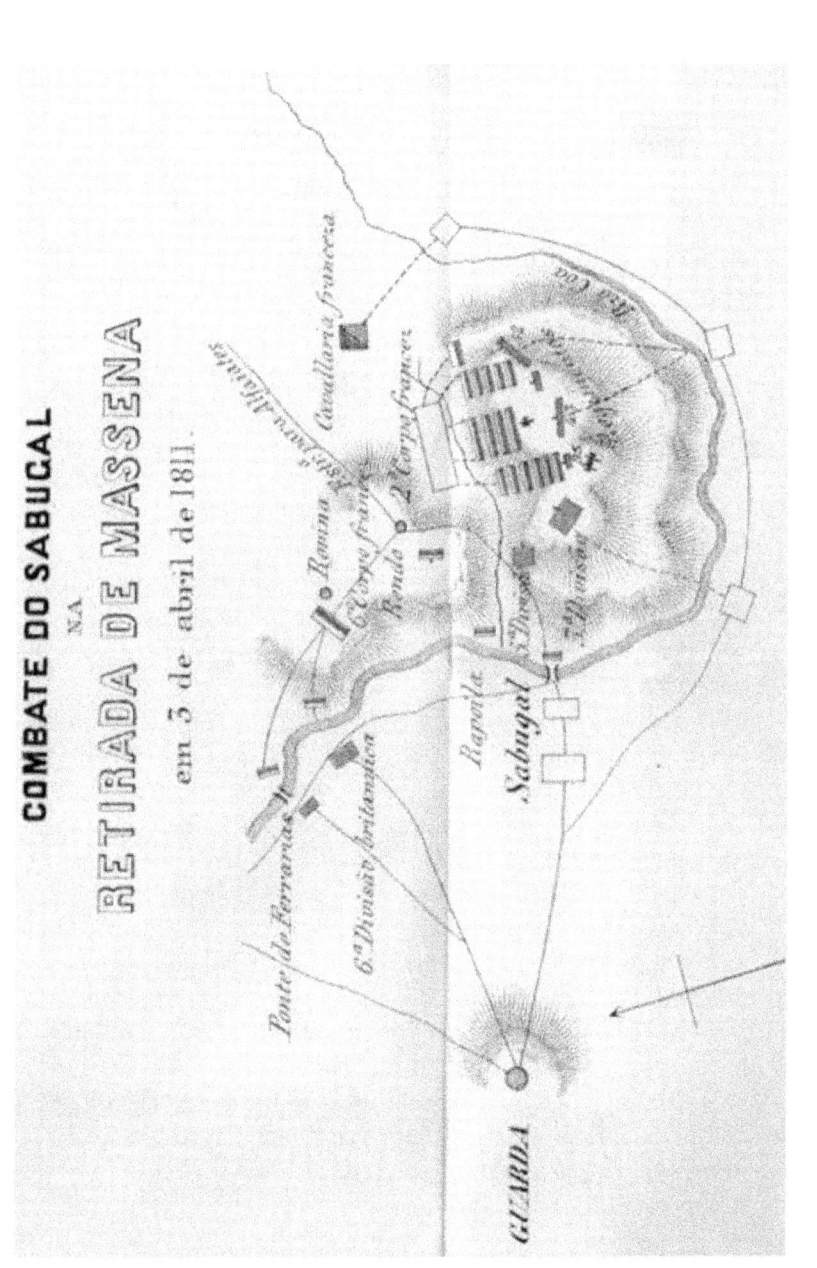

bank of the Agueda, at Villa del Egua in the Spanish province of Leon, and intelligence was brought in from the Spanish town of Ledesma to the effect that the French Army had been reinforced and reorganised, and that it was advancing. A squadron of the Fourteenth was hastily despatched under command of Captain Brotherton to Santa Esperita, but this was soon driven back behind the Agueda by the advancing columns of the enemy.

General Brotherton relates the following amusing anecdote with reference to the experiences of his patrol on this occasion:—

I had been sent (in May 1811) patrolling to a distance from the army, in search of the enemy, when we were behind the Agueda, and had not found him after a most harassing and fatiguing day, in most sultry weather, and could not get back to the army that night, but put up at San Felices, where I considered we were out of reach of the enemy. I put up at the priest's house, placing the men and horses, twelve in number, under sheds, in a large back yard, and felt so fatigued myself that I was tempted by the sight of a nice clean bed, and after a hearty supper which the priest gave me, to turn into bed, where I soon fell fast asleep. In the middle of the night I was woke by the priest coming to my bedside, and telling me that some French cavalry were passing through the town.

I jumped up, and went to the window, and, by the light of the moon, which shone brightly, sure enough, I saw French cavalry very composedly walking through the streets, and just commencing to billet off, knocking at the different doors, and at the same moment came a loud rap at the priest's door. I had not even time to put on my breeches, but scampered off with only my cloak and my sword, and got down just in time to jump on my horse, and get my party out of the back gate, and galloped off in an opposite direction to that which the enemy had come from. I was not followed, and the enemy changing his intention marched through the place without halting in it, so I returned to fetch my breeches, etc., and to thank the honest and hospitable priest who, though frightened at first, laughed heartily at my *sans culotte* adventure, which was matter of mirth throughout the army.

The object of this advance of the Prince of Essling was to relieve Almeida, which the allies had besieged. On 25th April he reached

Ciudad Rodrigo.

On the 3rd May, whilst we were retiring in the face of very superior numbers of the enemy, Lieutenant John Townsend [27] of the 14th Light Dragoons was in charge of the picquets, and he had to bring them in gradually under a heavy cannonade towards Fuentes d'Onor. The main body of the Fourteenth was engaged the same day behind Gallegos, and a squadron commanded by Captain Brotherton had a sharp skirmish near Poço Velho. Wellington had concentrated the main body of his army behind the Duas Casas River, and the French had to cross the Azava River, which was swollen and difficult to ford: this delayed them a few days, and the British advanced posts fell back on Fuentes d'Onor, where the main body occupied a tableland between the Turones and Duas Casas, their left being at Fort Conception, their centre opposite the village of Alameda, and their right behind Fuentes d'Onor.

On the 4th May, Wellington extended his right to Nave d'Aver, which, excluding the circuit of blockade round Almeida, made his line of battle 7 miles in length, but this gave him a safer line of retreat. Our cavalry was very weak at this battle, and the enemy was particularly strong in that arm: ours did not exceed a thousand sabres. The French attack commenced two hours after daybreak on the 5th May, by Montbrun turning the right of Wellington's Seventh Division, and then charging the British cavalry, which had moved up in support.

The attack made on our position in the rear of the village is thus alluded to by Napier:—

> The French with one shock drove in all the cavalry out-guards, and cutting off Captain Ramsay's battery, came sweeping in upon the reserves of horse and upon the Seventh Division. But their leading squadrons approaching in a disorderly manner, were partially checked by the British, and, at the same time, a great commotion was observed in their main body. Men and horses there closed with confusion and tumult towards one point, a thick dust arose, and loud cries, and the sparkling of blades, and the flashing of pistols, indicated some extraordinary occurrence.
> Suddenly the multitude became violently agitated, an English shout pealed high and clear, the mass was rent asunder, and Norman Ramsay burst forth at the head of his battery, his

---

27. Afterwards Colonel J. Townsend, A.D.C., commanding 14th Light Dragoons.

horses, breathing fire, stretched like greyhounds along the plain, the guns bounding behind them as things of no weight, and the mounted gunners followed in full career. Captain Brotherton of the 14th Dragoons seeing this, rode forth with a squadron and overturned the head of the pursuing troops, and General Stewart joining in the charge, took the French General Lamotte, fighting hand to hand.

After this the British cavalry had to retire behind the Light Division, which was thrown into squares. The Seventh Division fell back from Nave d'Aver, taking up a fresh position across the Turones River by Freneda, and during this retrograde movement the right flank was covered by the-14th Light Dragoons and the Royal Dragoons, who retired in good order by alternate squadrons under a heavy cannonade. One squadron of the Fourteenth charged some French artillery with great gallantry, but was repulsed, and it was here that Captain Knipe, commanding the squadron, fell mortally wounded, and was succeeded by Lieutenant (afterwards Colonel) John Townsend, who took command of the squadron. Lieutenant-Colonel Hervey at the head of the regiment had his horse killed under him, and received a severe contusion.

The following casualties were incurred in this battle by the Fourteenth:—

Killed:— Captain Knip,
4 men.
6 horses.
Wounded:— Lieutenant-Colonel Hervey.
Captain Milles.
Lieutenant Townsend.
Lieutenant Gwynne.
Lieutenant Badcock.
Lieutenant Ellis.
13 sergeants.
28 men.
23 horses.
Missing:— 3 men.
4 horses.

The Battle of Fuentes d'Onor was a hardly contested one. The French were superior in cavalry, having 5000 to our 1200, and having 40,000 infantry, 36 pieces of artillery, and a battery of the Imperial

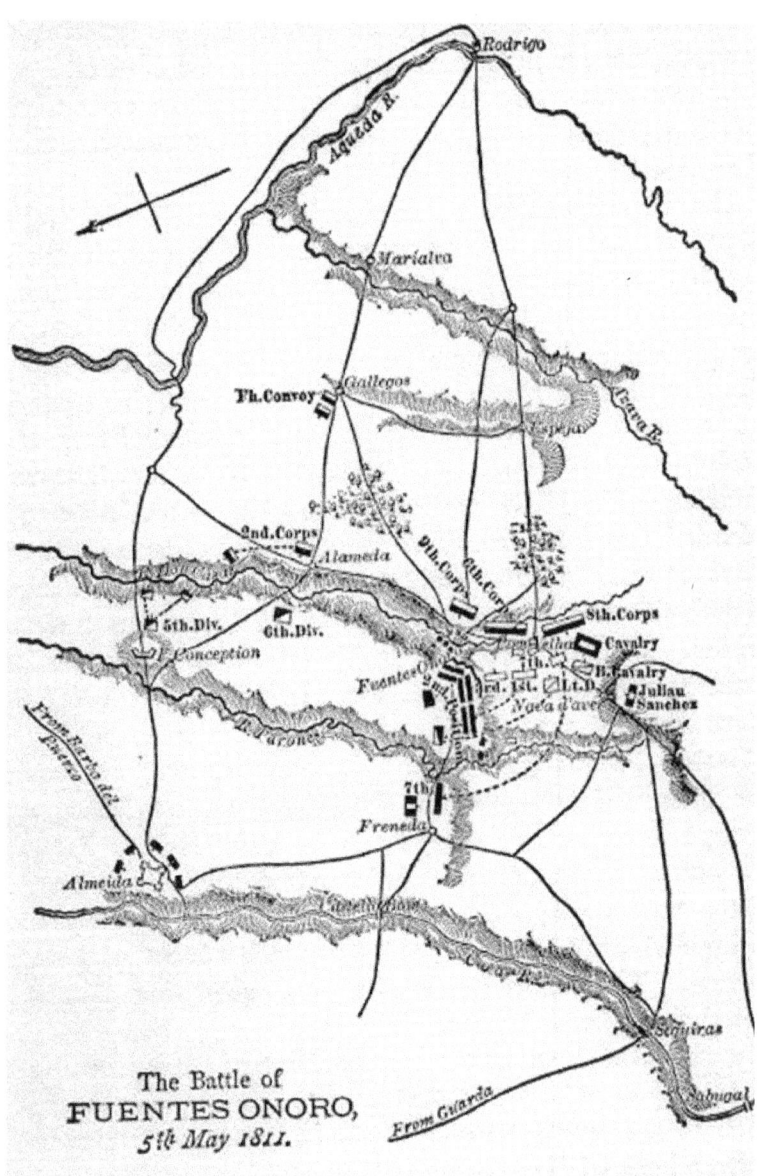

The Battle of
FUENTES ONORO,
5th May 1811.

Guard to our 32,000 infantry and 42 guns. What took place on our extreme right has already been described. At the same time, nearer the centre, and in front of the village of Fuentes d'Onor, a fierce battle also raged, and two companies of the 79th Regiment were taken, Colonel Cameron being mortally wounded.

It was here the French general, Drouet, made his furious attack on our lines, when he captured the lower part of the village notwithstanding the gallant stand made by the 71st, 79th, and 88th Regiments, who, though overmatched at first by sheer numbers and the fierce vigour of the attack, never quite relinquished the whole village, but rallied and then made a charge in which large numbers of the enemy fell. Here the fighting went on till evening, when the French at last retired some distance from the stream, and the British remained holding on to the crags and chapel.

On the extreme left, near Fort Conception, the allies maintained their position; and when at length the fighting, which had been desperate, came to an end, both armies remained as it were in observation the one of the other.

The total losses of the allies were 1500 men and officers, of whom 300 were taken prisoners. The enemy's loss was estimated at 5000, but this was over the mark. By the 10th May, Massena had retired beyond the Agueda, having been foiled in the attempt to relieve Almeida, and shortly afterwards Marmont assumed command of the French army operating towards Portugal. Both sides claimed a victory at Fuentes d'Onor, and Napier says, 'more errors than skill were observable on both sides' in this battle.

Lieutenant-Colonel Hervey received a gold medal, and the Royal authority was granted in 1820 for the Fourteenth to bear on its guidons and appointments the words 'Fuentes d'Onor,' as a special mark of His Majesty's approbation of the conduct of the regiment on this occasion.

General Brotherton relates several interesting episodes about Fuentes d'Onor:—

1. At Fuentes d'Onor the Adjutant-General of the army (Lord L——) was near me, particularly in one remarkable instance in which he joined in a charge I made to protect and rescue Captain Ramsay's guns of the Horse Artillery, as mentioned in Napier's *History*. At another period of the battle he ordered me to go to the assistance of Don Julian Sanchez, whose gueril-

las were getting roughly handled by some French cavalry. Of course I immediately obeyed, though it seemed to me an injudicious order, for on this memorable day our great inferiority in cavalry (the enemy having fully 4000 in the field of their very best, a large proportion of it of the Imperial Guard, and commanded by Montbrun, one of their best officers) rendered it advisable to keep the little we had constantly together, and detaching any of it to a distance a dangerous step.

However, as I before said, I instantly obeyed, and started at a brisk trot; for, in action, the least hesitation or slowness in executing an order is inexcusable in an inferior officer. I had not proceeded one hundred yards, when Lord Wellington, who was just arriving on this part of the field, rode up to me and asked me where I was going. I told him the orders I had received from Lord L—— (then General S.). He made no further observation than "Go back!"

2. At Fuentes d'Onor we had a very fine fellow, Captain Knipe, killed through his gallant *obstinacy*, if I may so call it. We had the night before been discussing the best mode for cavalry to attack batteries in the open field. He maintained, contrary to us all, that they ought to be charged in front, instead of the usual way in gaining their flanks, and thereby avoiding their fire. Poor fellow, the experiment next day, in support of his argument, was fatal to him. He had the opportunity of charging one of the enemy's batteries, which he did by attacking it immediately in front, and got through the discharge of round-shot with little loss; but the enemy having most rapidly reloaded with grape, let fly at his party, at a close and murderous distance, almost entirely destroying it; he himself receiving a grape-shot, passing through his body.

The shot went through his lungs. I was with the poor fellow the next morning, as long as he survived. He could speak distinctly, and was most composed and resigned, and even argued the point over again. His chief anxiety, however, was to be permitted to write a line to his mother, and he expired in the very act of attempting it. We buried him in the same grave with another gallant soldier who fell that day, Colonel Cameron of the 79th Highlanders.

3. Captain Badcock, commanding a squadron of the 14th Light

Dragoons, was sitting on his horse at the head of his adventure, squadron, when he took for Spaniards running away (a very usual occurrence) some cavalry rapidly approaching him in line, and remained perfectly steady, intending to charge those who appeared to be following the supposed Spaniards, the moment the latter had passed him. He was, however, not very agreeably surprised by being undeceived by a cut across the face from the French officer (for the supposed Spaniards were French). Badcock, however, who was an excellent officer, contrived, notwithstanding his surprise, to drive the enemy back in gallant style, with the loss, however, of two of his teeth; but he never thought of his wound till he had completed his duty, and then even never left the field for one moment.

4. Colonel Hervey, at the Battle of Fuentes d'Onor, escaped losing his right leg by having put a thick book (Quenedo's *Works*, which he had taken from a private house the day before) escape into his sabretache. An eight-pound shot entering the sabretache, went through the horse, and just appeared on the other side of his body, without coming through the skin, and it was evident that the thick book prevented it from going through and taking off Colonel Hervey's leg. Poor fellow, he had already lost his right arm; and his leg, from the blow, immediately swelled to an immense size, but though the horse fell down dead, and in the fall again hurt him, he would not leave the field, but had himself placed under a tree, where he remained during the remainder of the battle.'

5. It was either Fuentes d'Onor or the affair of Espeja,[28] near Ciudad Rodrigo, about which General Brotherton says:—
I had my charger shot under me, and got on a troop-horse which was also shot under me, through the head, by the pistol of a French officer, so closely that my own face was singed. The animal fell, and a sergeant behind me dismounted and gave me his horse, and I thought no more of the animal that was shot through the head, supposing that he never rose again; but on rejoining the main body of the regiment I found that the poor animal had arisen by an effort, gone back to where the regiment was formed, placed himself in the ranks in his own squadron, and then fell down dead! This fact, almost incredible,

---

28. Or Espejo (Cannon).

can be vouched for by any officer or private belonging to the 14th Light Dragoons at the time.

6. I commenced the Battle of Fuentes d'Onor by running away with 2 squadrons, for about 2 miles, pursued by a *brigade* of French cavalry. I had been sent the night before to the village of Nave d'Aver, which was occupied by that humbug, Don Julian Sanchez, with his corps of infantry and cavalry. It was a strong post, on an eminence, surrounded by stone wall enclosures, similar to those in Ireland, and no cavalry alone ought to have carried it. I arrived there late at night, and could not see what arrangements Don Julian had made for defence; but he assured me all was secure, and that he meant to defend himself most obstinately, before he retired. Just at daybreak in the morning, however, having requested him to show me where his picquets were posted, he pointed out to me what he said was one of them, but I observed to him that it appeared to me in the dusk of the morning too large to be one of his picquets, but he persisted.

However, the sun rising rapidly, as it does in these countries, dispelled the fog and the illusion the same moment, for what Don Julian pointed out to me as his picquet, proved to be a whole regiment of French cavalry dismounted. They mounted immediately and advanced. I still thought the Spaniards would make a stand, as cavalry alone never ought to have carried the village; but the *brave* Don Julian, as the Spaniards called him, took himself off immediately with his whole force to the mountains, and left me with my 2 squadrons to shift for myself. The consequence was that I was pursued by the whole French cavalry towards the position at Fuentes d'Onor, where the army was drawn up, and the advance-guard of which was at Poço Velho, which, as I approached, I saw occupied by red-coats, and began to breathe and feel secure.

As I approached I found our infantry posted with great regularity and steadiness, but as they did not commence firing on the French cavalry that were closely pursuing me, I rode up to the first officer I could approach, and asked him why he did not fire and stop the progress of the enemy. He replied with astonishment, "Are those the French?" I told him I knew it to my cost, having sustained considerable loss from them during my retreat.

He immediately commenced firing on them, and most effectually checked them, bringing down numbers of men and horses. I found this was the 85th regiment, only just come up to the army, and never having seen the enemy before. There was, however, no want of steadiness and bravery when once they were told it was the enemy. This gave me the liberty of retiring leisurely to the position where the army was drawn up, and the battle then commenced in earnest. At this battle the numerical superiority of the enemy, in cavalry, was *four to one*, and of the best description, a considerable proportion being cavalry of the Guard; and some of the most distinguished of the French cavalry generals were commanding it Montbrun, Fournier, etc. This was an eventful and critical battle.

We have thus seen how the attempt to relieve Almeida had signally failed; but on the night of the 10th May the garrison blew up the fortifications, destroyed the guns, and breaking through the picquets in one column, skilfully led by General Brennier, the governor of the fortress, made good their escape and joined the main body of the French army which then withdrew to Salamanca.

Lord Wellington now proceeded to Estremadura, leaving a large portion of his army on the Portuguese frontier, near Ciudad Rodrigo. The Fourteenth and Royal Dragoons, brigaded under Major-General Slade, took the outposts on the Agueda, covering the front between Villa del Egua, Gallegos, and Espeja.

Subsequently Marshal Marmont, Duc de Raguse, advanced once more with a numerous army and drove back the British posts from Ciudad Rodrigo, having introduced a convoy into the town. On the morning of the 6th June two French columns appeared, when the Light Division was directed to retire from Gallegos upon Nave d'Aver, and subsequently upon Alfayates. A squadron [29] of the Fourteenth acted with the Royal Dragoons under Lieutenant-Colonel Clifton to cover the retrograde movement. This retreat is described by General de Ainslie as follows, in his *Historical Record of the Royal Dragoons:*—

> The Royal Dragoons, under Lieutenant-Colonel Clifton, together with a troop of the 14th Light Dragoons, assembled at 3 a.m. at Gallegos for the purpose of covering the retreat. At 7 a.m. the enemy, numbering 2000 cavalry, 6000 infantry, and

---

29. Cannon, says it was a squadron, but General de Ainslie in his *Historical Record of the Royal Dragoons* says it was only a troop of the Fourteenth.

10 guns showed themselves, and this overwhelming force was met by the British cavalry in a most resolute and able manner. The celebrated French cavalry general, Montbrun, in vain endeavoured to outflank the Royals and 14th Light Dragoons. His squadrons were twice attacked and defeated, and the retreat of the Light Division was effected with little loss. Lieutenant-General Sir Brent Spencer, commanding the forces, in the absence of Viscount Wellington in Estremadura, thus reports to his lordship on these events:

> It is with the greatest pleasure I have to mention the very admirable conduct of 'the Royals' under the command of Lieutenant-Colonel Clifton, and one troop of the 14th Light Dragoons, which, being all that were employed in covering the front from Villa del Egua to Espeja, were assembled at Gallegos, and retreated from thence agreeably to my directions, and notwithstanding all the efforts of General Montbrun, who commanded the French cavalry, to outflank the British, pressing them at the same time in front with eight pieces of cannon. Their retreat to Nave d'Aver merits the highest commendation.

Marshal Marmont afterwards went to Spanish Estremadura with his large army, and the British general withdrew the troops he had in front of Badajos, and brought them to the vicinity of Ciudad Rodrigo, from which they had previously had to retire into Portugal. In the blockade of that city the Fourteenth took part as usual in the outposts, and when the French Army advanced to relieve the blockade the regiment was stationed at Espeja, on the lower Azava, with advanced posts at Carpio and Marialva. The French marshal managed to get supplies into Ciudad Rodrigo, and brought up such enormous forces that eventually the blockade was raised and the British had to fall back.

On the 23rd September, Marmont, advancing from Tamames, encamped behind the hills north-east of Ciudad Rodrigo. On the 24th the convoy entered the town, and 2 columns of French crossed the hills. On the same day Lord Wellington brought up a division of the allies to the position of Guinaldo, the rest of his army being disposed at various adjacent places such as Elbodon, Pastores, on the Vadillo (a river which falls into the Agueda, 3 miles above Rodrigo), Nave d'Aver, Espeja, and the lower Agueda.

On the 25th September, contrary to the British general's expectation, the French advanced from the Vadillo. Soon after daybreak 14 squadrons of the Imperial Guards drove the out-posts from Carpio across the Azava; the lancers of Berg at crossed the river in pursuit, but they were charged and driven back by a squadron of the Fourteenth and 2 squadrons of the 16th Light Dragoons, upon which Carpio was again occupied by the British. The same day another strong body of the enemy under Montbrun attacked the British at Elbodon, from which they had to retire, the Fourteenth also falling back from Carpio, and a succession of retrograde movements of the whole of the allies now took place, until on the morning of the 28th they took up a strong position in front of the Coa, their right resting on the Sierra de Mesas, their centre covered by the village of Soita, their left at Rendo, upon the river.

There had been frequent fighting during these three days without heavy losses on either side, and there were many brilliant instances of bravery and heroism in the actions at Carpio, Elbodon, and Aldea Ponte. In consequence of the unreturned fire at Elbodon, delivered by the infantry squares and the Portuguese artillery on the masses of French cavalry which charged the British so frequently and so vehemently, under Montbrun, the losses of the enemy were far greater than those of the allies. The Fourteenth had Lieutenant Hall, 2 private soldiers, and 5 horses wounded in the action at Carpio and the subsequent movements; and the conduct of the commanding officer, Lieutenant-Colonel Felton Hervey, was commended in public despatches, the excellent behaviour of Captain Brotherton being also mentioned. [30]

Marmont's army being very short of provisions, he took it back to the valley of the Tagus on the same day that the allies took up their position behind Soita. It was either during these movements or a day or two earlier at Espeja that the memorable affair between the Fourteenth and the enemy's lancers took place. The 14th and 16th Light Dragoons with the German Hussars were in brigade together under command of Count Arentschild of the German Hussars. The enemy's lancers ('The Polish Lancers'), a crack corps in the French cavalry, were observed drawn up on some rising ground, when Arentschild rode up to Lieutenant-Colonel Hervey and said, 'Sir, you will charge them.'

Two squadrons of the Fourteenth immediately advanced to the attack, the lancers awaiting them on their own ground with lances 'advanced,' thinking the Light Dragoons would never get inside them. However, the Fourteenth charged, broke through their ranks, and sa-

---

30. Cannon's *Historical Record of the 14th Light Dragoons.*

bred more than 60 of them. It is said the Fourteenth were offered lances as a compliment on their return after the war, but refused them, giving as a reason what occurred on this memorable occasion. It was always thought Count Arentschild wanted to spare his 'pet' German Hussars, and so sent the Fourteenth against the lancers.

Napier mentions a fine chivalrous act which took place at one of the many cavalry encounters which occurred during these three days' fighting with the enemy at Carpio, Elbodon, and Aldea Ponte: 'A French officer, while striking at Felton Hervey of the 14th Light Dragoons, perceived he had only one arm, and with a rapid change brought down his sword into a salute and passed on.'

In December of this year (1811) a schoolmaster-sergeant was for the first time appointed to the regiment. There were some reductions made in the establishment, *viz.*, the corporals were reduced from 50 to 40, the privates from 950 to 760, and the troop-horses from 964 to 864.

On 4th June, Colonel S. Hawker had been promoted Major-General on the staff at home, and Lieutenant-Colonel Hervey succeeded to the command of the Fourteenth, which he had virtually held since the death of Lieutenant-Colonel Neil Talbot a year previously. It was not till the year 1817 that Lieutenant-Colonel Hervey's name appeared in the Army List as the only Lieutenant-Colonel of the regiment, for in the Army Lists up to and including the year 1816, Major-General Hawker's name continued at the head of the regiment as Lieutenant-Colonel, though holding the rank of Major-General.

During the winter the strength of the regiment on foreign service was reduced from 8 to 6 troops. Accordingly, on 5th December 2 troops embarked at Lisbon for England, where they arrived on the 8th January 1812, and having disembarked at Portsmouth, joined the depot at Radipole Barracks, Weymouth.

Napier says that after the combats about Guinaldo, the allied army was extensively cantoned on both sides of the Coa.

Ciudad Rodrigo was distantly observed by the British, and so closely by Julian Sanchez, that he actually captured the governor, who had come out with too weak an escort, and also took a large number of oxen. In consequence of this the French Army under Thiebault, coming from Salamanca and Tamames, advanced when the Agueda was flooded, re-victualled Ciudad Rodrigo, leaving a new governor there, and returned on 2nd November before the waters had subsided; so that Wellington was unable to oppose him, the only bridge available being at Ciudad Rodrigo, in possession of the enemy.

Later in November the French made another advance under Dorsenne. The British and allies then crossed the Agueda near Zamara, whereupon the French retired, harassed in rear by the guerillas under Carlos d'España and Julian Sanchez.

After this, owing to want of supplies from the country between the Coa and Agueda, and the failure of the transport promised by the Portuguese, Wellington was forced to spread out his cavalry even as far as the Mondego and valley of the Douro, or they would have been starved. At this time the British Army was not in good plight. The last reinforcements received by Wellington consisted of infantry that had served in the recent Walcheren expedition, who were so enfeebled that exposure to night air or hardship at once threw them into hospital by hundreds, whilst the recently arrived cavalry regiments, being inexperienced and not acclimatised, were found, both men and horses, so unfit for duty that they had to be sent to the rear.

Added to this, the pay of the army was three months in arrear, the supplies were very scanty, half and quarter rations were often served; often there was no bread for three days consecutively, and the men's clothing was so patched that scarcely a regiment could be known by its uniform. Chopped straw, the only forage, was very scarce; the regimental animals were dying of hunger; corn was rarely distributed save to the generals and staff, and even the horses of the artillery and the old cavalry suffered. The cantonments about the Coa and Agueda were unhealthy from the rains; 20,000 men were in hospital, and only 54,000 men of both nations, including garrisons and posts of communication, were under arms.

But the change of position worked wonders: the new cantonments gave abundance of supplies and dry weather, for in Beira the first rains usually subside in December, and the sickness stopped in consequence. At this critical time the army was lucky in having such a capable military secretary as Lord Fitzroy Somerset.[31] It was now that Wellington decided to besiege with vigour and then to storm Ciudad Rodrigo on the first opportunity. He had 35,000 men available to do it with.

1812

Hitherto Ciudad Rodrigo had not been regularly invested, but on the 8th January the redoubt of Francisco was stormed and taken by selected companies of the Light Division led by Colonel Colborne,

---

31. Afterwards General Lord Raglan. (Napier, Book xvi. ch. 2.)

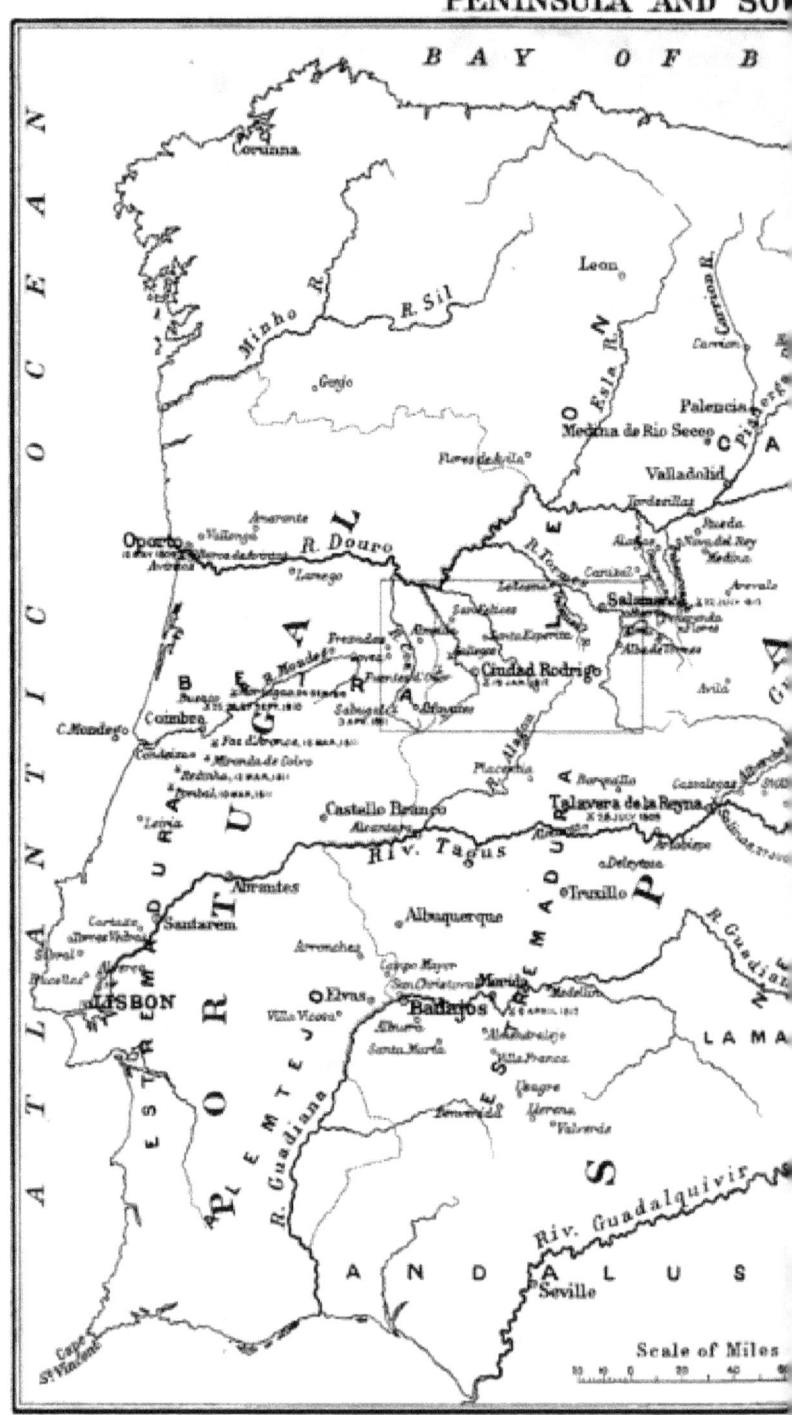

OF FRANCE 1808-1814.

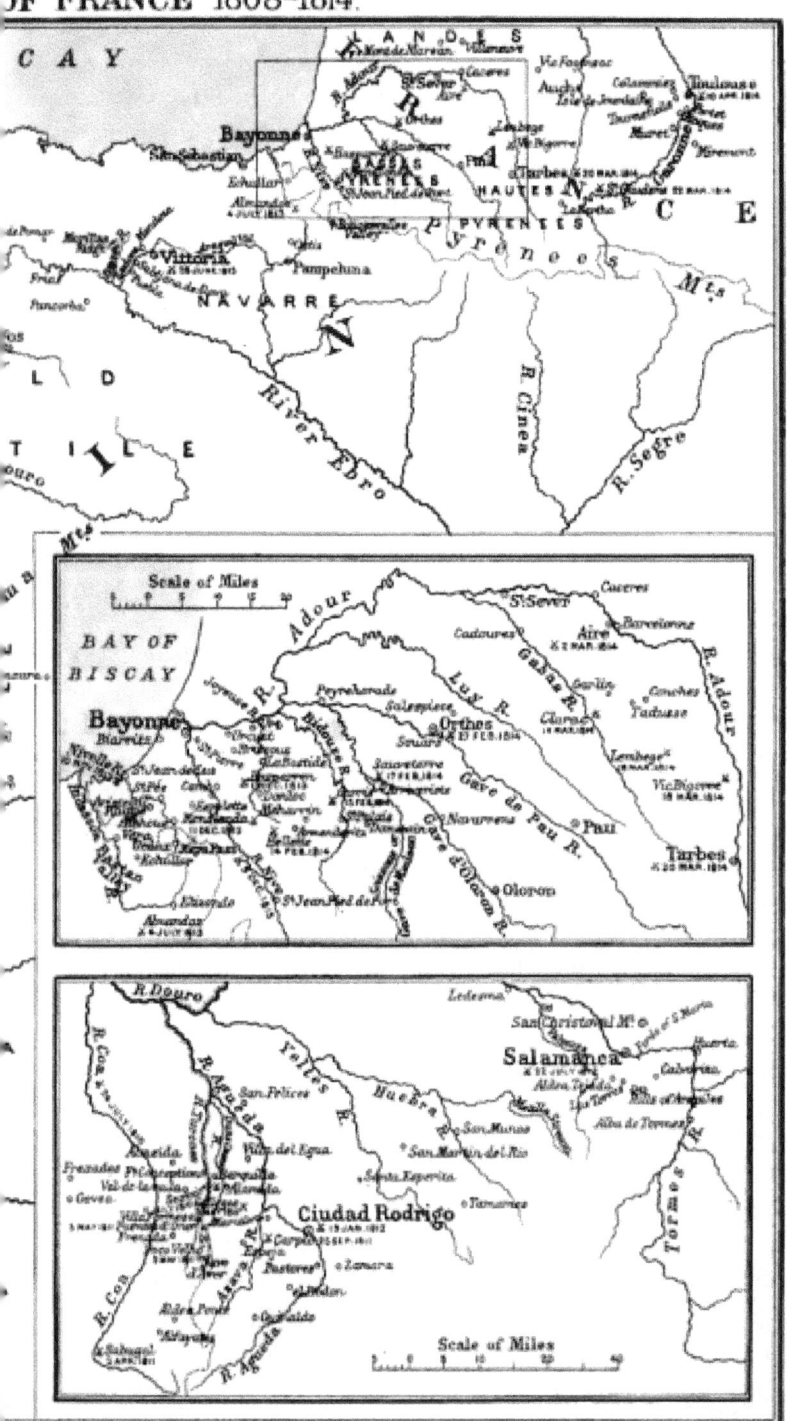

52nd Light Infantry, after which a regular siege and investment took place, and by the 19th two breaches became practicable. The assault, after desperate fighting and heavy losses, was successful. Lieutenant Gurwood, [32] one of the first to enter, received the governor's sword at the castle, though himself severely wounded in the head during the fight in the streets. Three hundred French fell, 1500 were made prisoners, 150 pieces of artillery were captured, and the allies lost 1200 men and 90 officers in the siege. Generals Craufurd and Mackinnon were killed.

It was a desperate affair: no less than 60 officers and 650 men were killed or hurt at the breaches. [33] After this gallant affair Lord Wellington was created Duke of Ciudad Rodrigo by the Spaniards, Earl of Wellington by the English, and Marquis of Torres Vedras by the Portuguese. The siege had lasted only twelve days, during which time the weather had been intensely cold with severe frosts, but from this time up to the end of February violent and continuous rain fell in the Peninsula. Ciudad Rodrigo was captured on the 19th January, and the garrison marched out as prisoners of war.

On the 30th January, Captain Charles Massey Baker (afterwards Lieutenant-Colonel of the Fourteenth), and on 26th March, Captain T. W. Brotherton (afterwards General Sir T. W. Brotherton, G.C. B.), became majors in succession to the Hon. C. Butler and J. Chapman. The cavalry had not taken any active part in the capture of Ciudad Rodrigo, but they were at hand in its vicinity to carry out reconnoitring duties as required, and to be in readiness for any unforeseen emergency.

After the place fell into our hands the British Army was kept on the Coa for some time, and Lord Wellington's headquarters remained there till 5th March, by which time the main body of his army was well on the way to the Alemtejo and the vicinity of Badajos, Marmont's army being at Salamanca. The Fourteenth proceeded to Estremadura, and was stationed near Badajos when the siege of that fortress commenced. The heavy rains which fell at the equinox considerably interfered with military operations, and in consequence the commencement of the siege was delayed till the 17th March.

The British headquarters were at Elvas by the 11th, and by the 15th pontoons were laid over the Guadiana River, and the investment of Badajos was completed soon after. There were several French armies hovering about: Soult was before the Isla, but Drouet's division, 5000

---
32. Lieutenant Gurwood, 52nd Regiment, led the forlorn hope. (Napier.)
33. Napier, from whose *History* this account of the siege is taken.

strong, was at Villa Franca, while Daricau, with a like force, was near Medellin; in consequence of which Lieutenant-General Sir Thomas Graham [34] was despatched with 3 divisions of infantry and 2 brigades of cavalry to march upon Llerena, by Valverde and Santa Marta, and Lieutenant-General Sir Rowland Hill was sent upon Almendralejos, moving thither from Albuquerque by Merida.

The Fourteenth were with the covering army under Sir Thomas Graham, and when the French Army under Marshal Soult advanced, the British fell back upon Albuhera. The regiment was employed in covering this retrograde movement, and it had an encounter, whilst skirmishing, with the enemy's advance-guard near Villa Franca, which is mentioned below. Badajos was captured by storm on the night of the 5th April, when the French relieving army fell back.

The Fourteenth were present at the siege of Badajos up to the 1st April, on which date they were relieved by the 11th Light Dragoons, and proceeded with the covering army under Sir Thomas Graham. Whilst in front of Badajos, on 20th March the garrison made a sortie, and two men of the Fourteenth were wounded.

After the fall of Badajos the Earl of Wellington proceeded to the north, but Lieutenant-General Sir Rowland Hill was left in command of the army in Estremadura. The British and Portuguese losses at Badajos were very heavy: it was a desperately contested assault. Five thousand men and officers fell in the siege, of whom, including 700 Portuguese, 3500 fell in the assault, 60 officers and more than 700 men being slain on the spot.

It was a few days after the capture of Badajos that the Fourteenth were engaged in an enterprise against several regiments of French cavalry. The regiments had moved on the night of the 10th April from Villa Franca upon Usagre, and afterwards along the road to Llerena. On the 11th the Light Brigade skirmished with the French, until the Heavy Brigade turned their flank. The enemy was then charged, overthrown, pursued, and many prisoners taken. On the night of the 12th April a party of the Fourteenth, under Lieutenant Edward Pellew, took a picquet of 22 French dragoons prisoners. The regiment had upwards of 20 men and several horses wounded in these affairs, and the conduct of Lieutenant-Colonel Hervey was commended in the despatch of the commander of the cavalry, Lieutenant-General Sir Stapleton Cotton, Bart.

The affair at Usagre was very skilfully managed by Sir Stapleton

---

34. Afterwards General Lord Lynedoch, G.C.B., G.C.M.G.

Cotton. Napier says the advance-guard of the Light Brigade commenced the action; the French fell back before Le Marchant's Heavy Brigade could intercept them, but as the heights skirting the Llerena road prevented them from seeing Le Marchant, they again drew up in order of battle behind the junction of the Benvenida road.

The numbers on each side were about 1900 sabres, and Cotton, seizing an accidental advantage of ground, kept the enemy's attention engaged with Ponsonby's (light brigade) squadrons, while Le Marchant, secretly passing at the back of the heights, sent the 5th Dragoon Guards against their flank, and the next moment Ponsonby charged their front. They gave way, and being pursued, lost several officers and 128 men prisoners, and many were killed in the field. The loss of the British was 56 men and officers, 45 being of the 5th Dragoon Guards. The French retreated on Drouet's infantry, then at Llerena, but all now fell back behind the Guadalquivir.

The French cavalry general was Peyrezmont, belonging to Soult's army. From Estremadura the Fourteenth marched towards the Agueda, and after being some time in Portugal and on the frontiers of Spain, formed the advance-guard of Sir Thomas Graham's column in the march towards Salamanca, near which city it skirmished with a body of the enemy on the 16th June, losing 1 sergeant and 1 trumpeter killed on that occasion, 4 privates and 5 horses of the regiment being wounded.

The French under Marshal Marmont retired beyond the Duero,[35] and the allies followed up to the banks of that river, where the 14th Light Dragoons were formed in brigade with the 1st German Hussars, and took the outposts at Tordesillas. The general advance of Wellington's army from the Agueda towards the Tormes commenced about the middle of June, when the rains ceased. His army numbered 24,000 men. He marched in 4 columns, and by the 17th June his army, now concentrated, occupied the mountain of San Christoval, 5 miles in advance of the city of Salamanca.

In the middle of July, on the 15th and 16th, Marshal Marmont with his large army commenced offensive operations against the allies, and crossed the River Duero at several points, so that Lord Wellington found it advisable to take up a position at Canizal, on the Guarena stream, where he united his centre and left, leaving Sir S. Cotton with the right wing (composed of the Fourth and Light Divisions and Anson's cavalry), on the Trabancos.

The French occupied Nava del Rey on the 17th, and on the same

---
35. Douro in Portugal, Duero in Spain.

day the Fourteenth and the 1st German Hussars, who had acted as rearguard and covered the retreat from Rueda behind the Guarena, moved to Alaijos so as to cover the retrograde movement of the right wing also, and Anson's cavalry from Castrejon. On the 18th some sharp skirmishing took place, and the troops at Castrejon fell back behind the Guarena. The Fourteenth had to retire from the plain near Alaijos under a heavy fire, and moved to Castrillos.

When the French Army came up to the opposite bank of the Guarena, General Clausel sent a brigade of cavalry under General Carier across, supported by a column of infantry, with the intention of attacking the British left. On this occasion Major-General Victor Baron Alten, commanding the brigade, led the 14th Light Dragoons and the 1st Hussars of the King's German Legion against the French cavalry, and some sharp encounters took place. Subsequently they charged the enemy's infantry most successfully. General Carier was taken prisoner, and the enemy was driven back. During this engagement the 27th and 40th Regiments, supported by a Portuguese brigade, broke the enemy's infantry by an impetuous bayonet charge after the Fourteenth and German Hussars had repulsed the cavalry, and it was now that our cavalry charged the broken infantry and sabred a number of them, pursuing and making some prisoners. The Fourteenth lost 18 men and 20 horses killed; 34 men and 18 horses wounded, as well as the following officers:—

Captain Brotherton.
Lieutenant John Gwynne.
Lieutenant Francis Fowke.

During the next three following days, the 19th, 20th, and 21st July, the regiment was actively employed in the operations which ensued between the opposing armies, and they had several skirmishes with the enemy.

On the 22nd July, at the Battle of Salamanca, the Fourteenth began at daybreak to skirmish with the French outposts, in company with the 1st German Hussars, acting as the advance-guard of the 3rd Division of Wellington's army, and they afterwards took their place in the line of battle. They were subsequently engaged successfully with the 3rd Division in its attack on the French left, when Major-General Victor Baron Alten was wounded. [36] The French commander, Mar-

---

36. The Fourteenth were in Alten's Brigade with the 1st German Hussars. After being shot in the thigh the brigadier was able to rejoin his brigade at Madrid six weeks later, and commanded it in the retreat to Salamanca and Portugal.

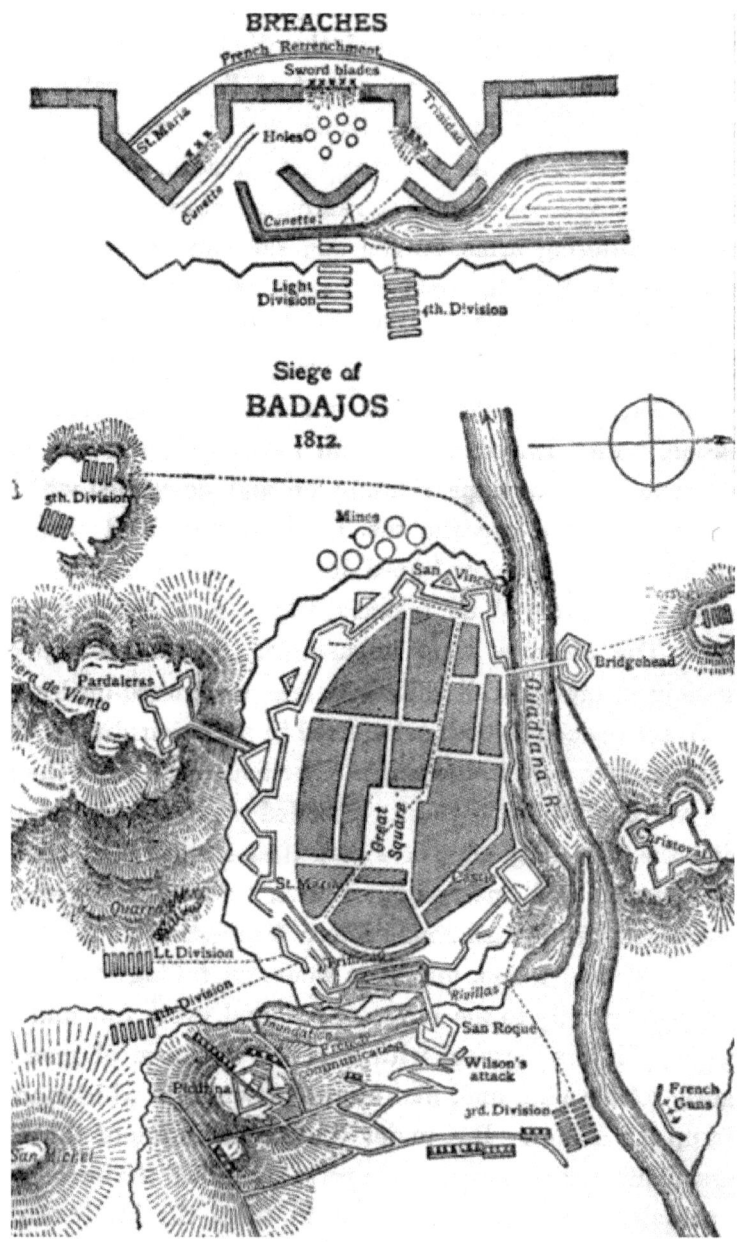

shal Marmont, endeavoured by several changes of position to turn our right, so as to gain the road leading to Ciudad Rodrigo. These movements occupied many hours, and it was near three o'clock in the afternoon when a report came to Wellington that the French left was actually pointing towards that road, and that it was rapidly moving away from the centre of the French Army.

He instantly repaired to the high ground and watched the movement intently for some time, and when at length he was quite satisfied that their left wing was entirely separated from their centre, he lost no time in taking advantage of such a flagrant fault in military tactics, and, ordering his divisions forward, commenced the battle in real earnest.

The allies' position had to be suddenly reversed from what it had previously been. In the first line as now constituted were the 4th Division, with the 5th on their right, Bradford's Portuguese on the right of the 5th Division, and Le Marchant's heavy cavalry on their right. In the second line were ranged the 6th and 7th Divisions, flanked on the right by Anson's light cavalry. This second line was now prolonged by the Spanish troops in the direction of the 3rd Division, which, with D'Urban's Portuguese cavalry, having passed the Tormes River by the fords of Santa Marta, was posted near Aldea Tejada, and so placed as to command the main road leading to Ciudad Rodrigo.

The allies' position having thus been reversed to what it originally was, their left now rested on the English Hermanito, their right on Aldea Tejada; the rear had become the front, and the interval between the 3rd and 4th Divisions was quickly filled by a simple countermarch, with Bradford's Portuguese infantry, the Spaniards and the British cavalry, all massed about the village of Las Torres.[37] Marmont's arrangements occupied several hours, he all the time masking his real intentions from the British commander, who had almost ceased to watch him until the false movement already alluded to was detected.

The 3rd Division was now reinforced by Arentschild's German Hussars, which, with D'Urban's horsemen, closed the extreme right at Aldea Tejada. A reserve, composed of the Light Division, Pack's Portuguese, Bock's and Alten's cavalry, remained in heavy masses on the highest ground behind all. The 3rd Division, with its cavalry and 12 guns, was ordered to advance and cross the enemy's line of march; the remainder of the first line, with the main body of the cavalry, was directed to advance whenever the attack of the 3rd Division was developed, while Pack's brigade was to assail the French Hermanito,[38]

---
37. Napier.

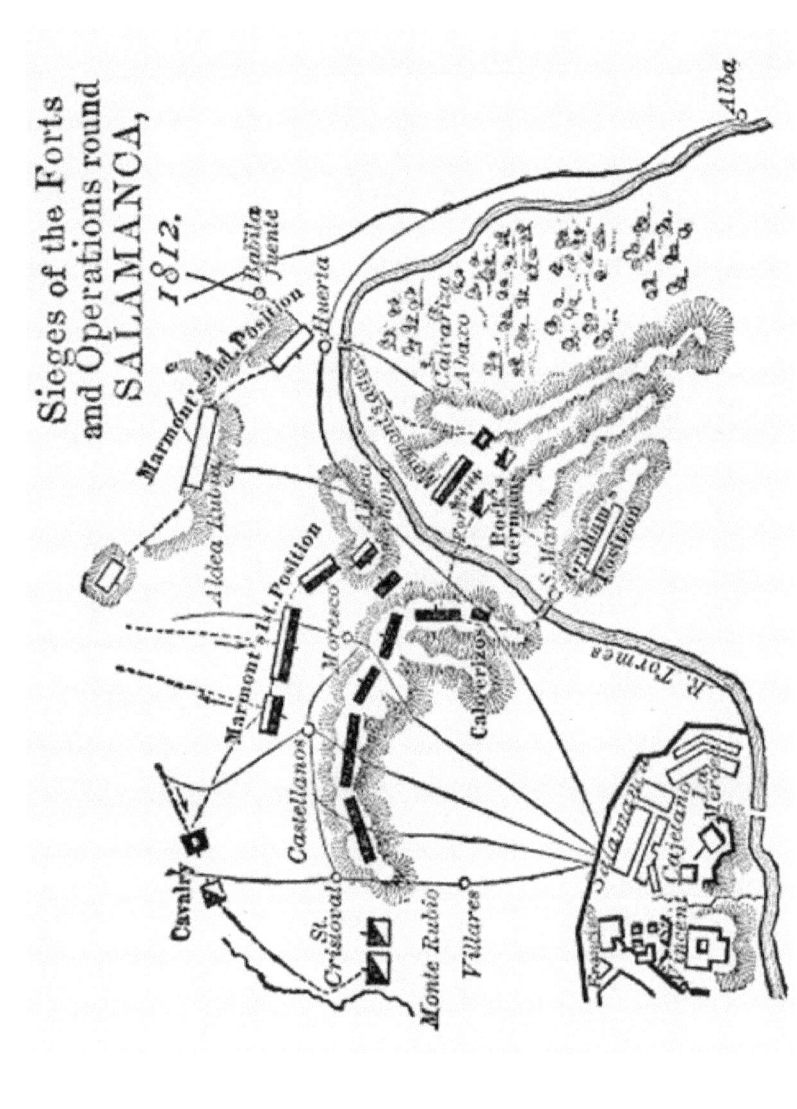

so soon as the left of the British line should pass it.

Marmont now used all his endeavours to hasten up his troops who were still behind, and at the same time to delay the progress of his left wing, and he was still hopeful of success until he observed Pakenham with the 3rd Division coming forward against his left; and it was when he was hurrying thither that he received a severe wound from an exploding shell which rendered him completely *hors de combat*. This contretemps had a serious effect upon the French troops, owing to the confusion which ensued in the giving of orders. Bonnet assumed command, but he too was soon after wounded, when Clausel succeeded him in the supreme command. It was about five o'clock when the 3rd Division fell upon the French left, commanded by Maucune and Thomières (the latter was killed); and two of our batteries of artillery, most skilfully posted on high ground, took them in flank. The French fought with great bravery, but the 3rd Division drove their opponents back in confusion upon the supporting columns.

It was just at this juncture the French cavalry assailed the flank of the 3rd Division, and were most gallantly charged by D'Urban's and Arentschild's horsemen, on which occasion the Oporto regiment under Watson attacked a square of infantry unsuccessfully and retired, leaving Watson wounded on the ground. [39] The Fourteenth were present with the 3rd Division in this important attack, which led to the complete discomfiture of the enemy's left; and two squadrons under Lieutenant-Colonel Hervey reinforced D'Urban's Portuguese Brigade, and thus took an active part in the successful turning movement which was effected. In the result, this repulse of the French left flank contributed more than anything else to our glorious victory at Salamanca, whereby the enemy was defeated with great loss and driven from the field.

Whilst this movement had been going on, the 4th and 5th Divisions and Bradford's Brigade were hotly engaged, but steadily gaining ground; Le Marchant's heavy cavalry, Anson's light cavalry, and Bull's troop of artillery were advancing at a trot upon the left of Pakenham's Division, whilst, as already related, on Pakenham's right D'Urban's cavalry had turned the disordered masses of the enemy's left. Although not more than half an hour had elapsed since the actual battle com-

---

38. There were two rugged hills on the field of battle called the Hermanitos or Arapiles. One was christened the 'English' and the other 'Marmont's' or the 'French Hermanito.'

39. Napier.

menced, the French were already losing ground, their left being in complete confusion.

They began to fire at random; and when the British cavalry charged forward, coming between the interval of the 3rd and 5th Divisions, and then forming line, Le Marchant's heavy horsemen and Anson's Light Brigade were seen to break forth at full speed, and next moment 1200 French infantry were trampled down by the charging squadrons, who rode onwards, sabring hundreds of them with their long straight swords. In this onslaught the cavalry lost heavily, Le Marchant and many other officers fell; Cotton and his staff were still at their head and galloped on, though opposed to a terrible fire; and Lord Edward Somerset, who persistently continued the charge at the head of one squadron, captured five guns.

The heavy cavalry met with the greatest opposition and suffered in proportion. Anson's Light Brigade had suffered little in the charge, so they still pressed on, joined by D'Urban's horsemen, and, united with the 3rd and 5th Divisions and the guns, engaged the enemy with vigour. Meanwhile a fierce battle raged in the centre also. There Clausel made a surprising effort. Our 4th Division had driven back Bonnet's troops, who got mixed with the disordered masses of Maucune's and Clausel's Divisions, now retreating before Pakenham and the cavalry. The French Hermanito was assailed, but unsuccessfully, by Pack's Portuguese about the time of Le Marchant's charge.

Clausel, when he assumed the command of the army, brought up Ferey's Division from Calvariza, and concentrated it in the centre behind Bonnet's troops, who were still strongly fighting; he also brought towards the same point the light cavalry, Boyer's dragoons, and the two divisions so long expected from the forest. By these dispositions he presented a mass for the broken left wing to rally upon, and he caused Sarrut's, Brennier's, and Ferey's unbroken divisions, supported by the whole of the cavalry, to cover the line of retreat to Alba de Tormes, while another division was in mass close behind Marmont's Hermanito, and Foy remained still intact on the right.

Pack had failed to take the Hermanito with his Portuguese: he was driven back by the French reserves hidden from view behind the rocks on his front and left flank; this was a very critical moment in the battle. The men of the 4th Division were also driven back from the southern ridge, and were menaced by Clausel's troops in rear and on their left, when the gallant 40th Regiment,[40] wheeling about, with a rough charge cleared the rear, and thus saved that quarter. The front of the 4th Division was, however, driven back, as well as the front line of the 5th, which Dover's dragoons had menaced. Cole had fallen, also Leith, both severely wounded; Beresford brought up some Portuguese troops, but he fell desperately wounded; and Boyer's dragoons now charged with success, in consequence of Anson's cavalry having been checked by a heavy fire of artillery.

This was the real crisis of the battle. Wellington now brought up the 6th Division from the second line, which made a well-sustained and vehement charge, losing heavily; Hulse's Brigade on the left lost hundreds, the 61st and 11th Regiments being exposed to a withering fire. The Fifty-Third were disordered by an impetuous charge of Boyer's dragoons and lost many men, but bravely held their ground. The fighting still continued, and the changing current of battle now turned for the British. Clausel, however, skilfully protected a line of retreat by the roads leading to the fords of Huerta and Encina, and the road leading to Alba de Tormes. Thither, accordingly, the French Army, driven by the 3rd, 5th, and 6th Divisions, fell back in disorder. Wellington assailed Foy's Division, which was covering the retreat, with his Light Division and some cavalry, supported by the 1st Division and two brigades of the 4th Division, whilst as a reserve he sent the Spaniards and the 7th Division.

The French retired by alternate wings in good order before these troops, firing upon the Light Division from every rise of ground, and this retrograde march continued for two miles, but luckily, owing to the twilight which baffled the French aim, our casualties were not large. Just before it became dark, however, the 6th Division was involved in a fight with Maucune's Division, and attacked a strong position, when they lost heavily from the fire of the French guns; but eventually the enemy got completely under cover of the forest and were lost to view, when the battle came to an end, and the French made good their retreat to Alba.

In this battle, Captain Brotherton of the 14th Light Dragoons, who, when fighting on the 18th July at the Guarena amongst the foremost, as he was always wont to do, [41] had a sword thrust through his side; yet he was again on horseback on the 22nd, and being denied leave to remain in that condition with his own regiment, secretly joined Pack's Portuguese in an undress, and was again hurt in the unfortunate charge at the Hermanito.

---

40. Now the South Lancashire Regiment, 1st Battalion.
41 Napier, vol. iv.

The casualties of the Fourteenth were not great at Salamanca—they had 4 men killed, and 6 men and 7 horses wounded.

After the battle Clausel passed the Tormes by the narrow bridge of Alba and the fords below it, and at daylight was in full retreat upon Penaranda. Wellington, having brought up his German dragoons and Anson's cavalry, also crossed the river with his left wing at daylight, and came upon the rear of the French Army near the Almar, a small river at the foot of a height near the village of La Serna. The cavalry pursued and attacked some squares of infantry, whom they took by surprise, and gained a success, but lost a hundred of their number killed by the fire of the French muskets.

The Light Division also came up and pursued to Nava de Setroval, near which place such large bodies of the French cavalry covered the rear of the army, that the allied cavalry, who were reduced in numbers and fatigued with fighting and marching, did not make any further attack, and the French made good their retreat in the direction of Flores de Avila and Arevalo. The Fourteenth were in the pursuit on 23rd July, when two squadrons of the regiment had a sharp engagement and took several prisoners near Penaranda.

The total losses of the allies at Salamanca and in the operations before and after the battle amounted to—

1 Field-marshal; 4 generals; and nearly 6000 officers and men killed and wounded. [42]

The losses of the opposing French Army during the same period, 18th to 30th July, were:—

1 Marshal; 7 Generals; and 12,500 men and officers killed, wounded, and taken.

The French also lost two eagles, several standards, twelve guns, and eight carriages. [43] It was on the 18th July that Marmont's army crossed the Duero in its advance, and on the 30th it recrossed that river in retreat, and finally had to retreat to Burgos, when the allies took possession of Valladolid.

For its gallant bearing at Salamanca the Fourteenth received the

---

42. The British lost 1 general killed Le Marchant; 5 generals wounded Beresford, Cole, Leith, Cotton, and Alten. The French lost, killed, 3 generals of brigade Thomières, Farey, and Desgraviers; wounded, Marmont and Bonnet, severely, and Clausel, slightly. The French Marshal Marmont had with him 44,000 men. He was joined on 8th July by Bonnet from the Asturias, and later by King Joseph from Madrid.
43. The account of the Battle of Salamanca is mostly taken from Napier.

royal authority in 1820 to bear the word 'Salamanca' on its guidons and appointments, and Lieutenant-Colonel Sir F. B. Hervey, Bart, received a gold medal in recognition of his services, and as a mark of royal favour and approbation.

It was on the 26th July that a patrol of 3 dragoons of the Fourteenth, and 4 men of the German Hussars, under Corporal William Hanley of the 14th Light Dragoons, detached to Blasco Sancho, captured a party of the enemy, consisting of 2 officers, 1 sergeant, 1 corporal, and 27 mounted dragoons, with 1 private servant and 2 mules with baggage, when they had been sent forward to observe the movements of the enemy. Corporal Hanley and his gallant patrol were most highly complimented by the Commander of the Forces, who himself, through Lieutenant-Colonel Sir F. B. Hervey, Bart., at Madrid, presented a pecuniary reward for the men of the patrol, and Corporal Hanley afterwards received a special medal for his gallantry.

The French horses were given to the Fourteenth and the German Hussars to complete deficiencies. The men captured by Hanley's patrol had really been left there by King Joseph of Spain, who had quitted Madrid on 21st July, and was at Blasco Sancho on the 24th, and thence made a forced march to Espinar.

The following extract from Tancred's *Historical Record of Medals* has reference to Corporal Hanley's medal:

> Corporal William Hanley, 14th Light Dragoons, was presented by the officers of his regiment with a silver medal at a full dress parade, as an honourable testimony and to commemorate a brave action. The medal bears on
> *Obverse* (within a wreath)
> Fortitudine Blasco Sancho, 26th July 1812. Peninsula.
> *Reverse* (within a wreath)
> William Hanley, Corporal, 14th Light Dragoons.

This medal was in the late Stewart Mackenzie's collection, but is now, (1901), in that of Major-General the Hon. Herbert Eaton, late Grenadier Guards.

General Brotherton relates some interesting episodes concerning events which happened at Salamanca, both before and after the battle, as follows:—

> The river called Douro in Portugal, is called Duero in Spain. When, in the summer of 1812, Lord Wellington and Marshal Marmont were manoeuvring against each other on the banks

of this river, towards Tordesillas, the river being much swollen by rains, it became essential, but very difficult to ascertain the fords, in order for one party or the other to know where to cross, either to attack or defend the passage. As the picquets of the respective armies were placed close to the banks, it was a ticklish thing to attempt the trial of any ford. I was determined, however, to attempt it, and had recourse to a little ruse in order to accomplish it. I rode out one evening late, with my orderly dragoon behind me, to the border of the river on the left bank, on which side the British Army was then posted, and immediately opposite to a French picquet. I crossed the river and found out the ford.

The French picquet looked on most composedly, thinking, no doubt, that myself and my orderly were deserters, and when we reached the opposite bank the French officer came up to me, and asked what we were and what we wanted. He advanced about fifty yards from his picquet, which was drawn out. I saw that it was necessary to get out of the scrape by stratagem, and I gave him some vague reply, upon which he seized hold of my bridle, perceiving that he had been humbugged by allowing me to cross the ford. I immediately drew my pistol, cocked it, and might have shot him dead, but did not like to commit such an act in cold blood. He staggered back and ran to his picquet, which he ordered to fire.

I had to dash into the river again, and in the hurry mistook the direction of the ford, and had to swim back across, during which time, the river being broad, myself and orderly had to undergo a very sharp fire of musketry. The trumpeter was shot through the body, and kept howling aloud till we reached the opposite shore. Thus I succeeded, though at no little risk, to ascertain what it would have cost the lives of many men to have ascertained by force, and I believe I got some credit for this act.

The first time we entered Salamanca I was commanding the advanced guard, and we gave a "View halloo" when we came within sight of the town which so astonished the French skirmishers with whom we were engaged that they took it for the "Hurrah" of a charge, and went back rapidly. I had an encounter, in single combat, this day with a very young French officer, between the two lines of skirmishers, French and English, who stood still, by mutual consent, to witness it.

The French officer showed great cunning and skill, seeing the superiority of my horse, for he remained stationary to receive me, and allowed me to ride round and round him, whilst he remained on the defensive. He made several cuts at the head of my horse, and succeeded in cutting one of my reins and the forefinger of my bridle-hand, which was, however, saved by the thick glove I wore, though the finger was cut very deeply to the joint.

As my antagonist was making the last cut at me, I had the opportunity of making a thrust at his body which staggered him, and he made off. I thought I had but slightly wounded him, but I found, on inquiry the next day, when sent on a flag of truce, that the thrust had proved mortal, having entered the pit of his stomach. I felt deeply on this occasion and was much annoyed, as I had admired the chivalrous and noble bearing of this young officer. He was a mere youth, who, I suppose, thought it necessary to make this display as a first essay, as French officers usually do on their first appearance in the field, and indeed, I believe it is expected of them by their comrades. I shall never forget his good-humoured, fine countenance during the whole time we were engaged in this single combat, talking cheerfully and politely to me, as if we were exchanging civilities instead of sabre-cuts.

There was a singular coincidence this day. We, the *14th Light Dragoons*, wore an *orange* facing, and the French regiment to which we were opposed proved to be the *14th French Chasseurs*, and also wore an *orange* facing. The cut I received on the forefinger of my bridle-hand proved a great grievance for some time, as it prevented me from playing the violin for weeks a great deprivation, as I always played in bivouac at night.

Early in the morning we found ourselves (that is General Alten's brigade, composed of the 14th Light Dragoons and 1st Hanoverian Hussars) in presence of a very superior force of the enemy's cavalry, with whom we commenced skirmishing, and who drove us back across the Guarena stream, a small river with steep banks. When we had crossed this stream with the whole brigade, we formed and waited till the enemy had crossed also, and then attacked him in "succession of squadrons from the right."

The two first squadrons that charged failed to make an impression on the enemy, and were repulsed. In leading the third squadron to the charge (which was mine), I was run through the body, from the right side to the navel, about six inches. When the point of the sword came out, and as I staggered and fell, my antagonist, instead of withdrawing his sword from my body altogether, drew it up a little and then made another thrust, which went into the cavity of my chest. I was then led off the field faint and sick, and I well remember one of my best old soldiers offering his assistance. He was wounded also, but said "it was nothing, only a little stab in the stomach."

Such, however, is the mortal nature of wounds with the point (the regiment we had charged was a heavy cavalry one with straight swords), that the poor fellow, as he was leading me off the field, suddenly staggered, vomited blood, and fell down dead. I must mention that I received my wound in the act of uplifting my arm and making a cut at the head of my antagonist, on his near side. He wore a brass helmet, and the blade of my sabre broke in two on it, which left me quite at his mercy.

I forgot to mention that, in the early part of this eventful day to me, the enemy cannonaded us when we were formed in line, and the mare I rode, a most valuable one, a pure Arabian of the highest caste, and known to the whole army for her great beauty, had her thigh shattered by a shell which fell close to me and burst. I immediately dismounted one of the troop-sergeant-majors and took his horse, sending him to the rear. She was at first considered so desperately wounded that I was advised, and was on the point of shooting her, but she afterwards miraculously recovered, and I was taken prisoner on her on the 13th December 1813, when her head was cut open.

I was bled twice, profusely, during the night, as the effects of inflammation were apprehended, these sort of wounds never bleeding much of themselves. I was, of course, much weakened, but determined not to lose the glorious Battle of Salamanca, which took place on the 22nd instant. I got on my horse, having slept in the town of Salamanca on the previous night, and I joined my regiment (in the field), which I found on the point of being engaged. I remained with it only a short time, as Colonel Hervey threatened to put me under arrest if I did not quit the field immediately, conceiving I was not in a fit state to remain. I left the regiment. It was, however, impossible to quit such a field at such a moment, and I repaired to the Arapiles hill, of which we then had possession, the enemy occupying the other immediately in front of it.

General Packe's brigade being ordered to attack the latter, and perceiving one of the Portuguese regiments giving way, I could not resist the temptation of attempting to rally them, and rode down to the valley for that purpose, but my horse was shot under me, and in the very weak state I was in, I felt very unequal to further exertion. Still, it was impossible to leave such a field at such a moment, and I remained to the last, having joined in the very last attack made by the 6th Division on the rocky heights to which the French had retired before they entirely gave way, and retreated.

This was late in the evening, and quite dark. I returned to Salamanca that night, where I slept, but started early next morning, looking like a ghost, and overtook the army pursuing the enemy. I was, however, obliged to lie down and rest every quarter of an hour. When I reached my regiment Colonel Hervey again remonstrated against my remaining with it, but my wound beginning to suppurate and do well, the surgeon said there was no risk, and I remained. We marched to Madrid, driving the enemy before us, and entered this romantic place amidst such enthusiasm on the part of the inhabitants, that it was more like a tale in the Arabian Nights than reality.'

At the Battle of Salamanca only two generals in the field were more than forty— the duke himself and another.

During the war in the Spanish Peninsula, in 1812, a patrol of four men of the 14th Light Dragoons (now the 14th Hussars), and four men of the 1st German Hussars, under a man whose name was Hanley, and whose rank I will tell you by and by, entered a village which some French soldiers they were watching had left shortly before. The patrol rode through the village, and on arriving at the further end saw three French dragoons returning from foraging, and making for a house standing by itself in the plain. Galloping after them, the patrol took them prisoners and then rode towards the house. From each end of the house ran a rather high wall forming a courtyard, with a stable in rear, but the only entrance was through the door of the house, and a narrow passage. The door was closed, but was opened by firing into the lock. Inside were French dragoons feeding their horses and preparing them for night.

Hanley made his men fire quickly down the passage so as to make the French believe his party was numerous. At this moment the French officer in command of the post suddenly fired at Hanley, through a window on the ground floor, but when Hanley was about to return the compliment, the Frenchman surrendered. He was made to give up his sword and pistol, and as the only way out of the room was into the passage, he would have been sure to be killed had he tried to escape.

One of the Germans of the patrol, who could talk French, was then sent with the French officer into the court to tell the French that they had better surrender, because the English cavalry brigade was coming, and unless they surrendered at once the thatched roof would be set on fire, and all in the place burnt to death. After a few minutes, the French officer and the German hussar returned, saying the men agreed to surrender.

The prisoners were ordered to leave their sabres in the courtyard, and come out one by one through the narrow passage, leading their horses. The passage was only broad enough for one man at a time. As each came out his carbine was taken from him, the stock broken and the pieces thrown away. One by one they came out, twenty-seven in all. Imagine their disgust when they found only nine English and German soldiers outside! They were made to mount their horses and cross their stirrups, then they marched off in fours, three of the escort on one side, four on the other, and Hanley and one trooper bringing up the rear, the French officer riding alongside Hanley, who held his reins for him.

This party had just left the house, when up came from some French troops on their march to this place a French lieutenant-colonel. He had seen the party from a distance, and thought they were English prisoners. Slapping Hanley on the shoulder as he passed him, he called out, "Good-day, Englishman," but before he knew where he was Hanley had whipped the Frenchman's sword out of its scabbard and made him prisoner. Then came up the colonel's orderly with a couple of mules with the colonel's baggage, and they all had to join the party, which after a march of some dozen miles rejoined the brigade.

The march of the army to Madrid now took place, the 14th Light Dragoons being in brigade with the 1st German Hussars (Hanoverians). The Marquis of Wellington himself entered Madrid on the 12th August, but the Fourteenth passed Segovia in Old Castile and bivouacked near Escurial, which is 26 miles north-west of the Spanish capital, where there is the magnificent palace built by Philip II. and used as a monastery. The headquarters of the regiment were established at Getafe, and the men were employed in outpost duty. Lieutenant Cust commanded a post of observation at Consingia, in La Mancha, and Lieutenant Ward was with a post of communication between that place and Madrid.

When the Marquis of Wellington left Madrid for the siege of Burgos, the regiment remained on for some time in the vicinity of the capital; but about the 24th of October, when, owing to a concentration of the French armies under King Joseph, Soult, and other marshals, the siege of Burgos was raised and a retiring movement forced upon the allies, the 14th Light Dragoons with the 1st German Hussars assembled at Guadalaxara, fell back on Madrid, and formed part of the rearguard of Lieutenant-General Sir Rowland Hill's Corps from thence to Alba de Tormes. For several days the Fourteenth were constantly engaged in manoeuvring and skirmishing to retard the advance of the enemy. The French moved upon Arevalo, Fontiveros, and thence to Alba de Tormes. Wellington coming from Burgos reached San Christoval, near Salamanca, on the 6th November.

At this time the king and his marshals had an army of 90,000 combatants on the Tormes, mostly veteran troops, of whom 12,000 nearly were cavalry, and they had 120 guns. Wellington had 68,000 combatants, and 70 guns. On the 14th November the French crossed the Tormes and took post at Mozarbes. The next day Wellington began his retirement towards Portugal on Ciudad Rodrigo, finding the French were too strong for him. He moved away in three columns across the Junguen,[44] and then, covering his left flank with his cavalry and guns, defiled in order of battle before the enemy at little more than cannon-shot.

Owing to a thick fog and heavy rain which was all in his favour, having possession of the high roads, while the enemy had only the fields and by-ways, he was enabled to bring his whole army in one mass quite round the French left, and gained the Valmusa River. This dangerous movement was rendered necessary owing to the time that

---
44. A rivulet running into the Tormes opposite Salamanca.

had been lost by the allies whilst they waited on the Arapiles at Salamanca, and thus allowed the French under Soult to cross the Tormes and turn their position.

On the 16th the allies retired by the three roads which led across the Matilla stream through Tamames, San Munos, and Martin del Rio, the Light Division and cavalry closing the rear. The 14th Light Dragoons, as before, still took part in the picquets and other duties of the rearguard, all through this retirement of the allies from Salamanca to Ciudad Rodrigo; and until the army went into cantonments behind the Agueda, they continued to perform them. The surrounding country was one huge forest filled with vast herds of swine. For two days the number of our stragglers was enormous, for the hungry soldiers, who were very short of rations and supplies, broke away by hundreds from their colours to shoot the wild pig, and the forests resounded with the roll of musketry as if the enemy were attacking. Lord Wellington took stringent measures to enforce discipline, and had two men hanged, but even so the soldiers did not desist, and in consequence there were no less than 2000 stragglers of Wellington's army taken by the enemy.

On the 16th November, when near Matilla, the French lancers pressed our rearguard hotly, but were checked by the light companies of the 28th Regiment, and were afterwards gallantly charged and driven back by the 14th Light Dragoons under Lieutenant-Colonel Sir F. B. Hervey, Bart., who again distinguished himself and was nearly made a prisoner, the enemy being in very superior numbers. The Fourteenth lost 1 corporal and 2 horses killed; 1 man wounded and 1 taken prisoner.

On the 17th, a large body of the French cavalry[45] surprised the picquets in front of the Light Division. The division was immediately formed in columns: a squadron of the Fourteenth and one of the German Hussars came hastily up from the rear, Julian Sanchez's cavalry, in small parties, formed on the right flank, and all precautions were observed to secure the retreat. This checked the enemy from making an attack, but his squadrons rode up near the flanks of our retreating infantry, and a good deal of baggage was taken and several men killed and wounded, nor did the enemy desist till finally driven off by our artillery. The French succeeded in taking General Paget prisoner as he was riding in the midst of his own men, concerning which Napier remarks that it might have been Wellington who was captured, for he also was continually riding between the columns and without an

---

45. Seventeen squadrons.

escort.

Soon after this the main body passed the Huebra, where the Light Division was assailed again by Soult's troops, but effected its passage with small loss. On the 18th, after a long and tiring march, Wellington reached Tamames, and next day Rodrigo and the neighbouring villages were occupied. This retreat beginning at Burgos had cost the allies a large number of men in killed, wounded, stragglers, and missing, besides prisoners captured by the enemy, as well as a large quantity of looted baggage. Victor Alten's Brigade of Cavalry, in which were the Fourteenth and the 1st and 2nd German Hussars, was attached to the Light Division and remained behind the Agueda, Captain Badcock being detached with a reconnoitring party from the regiment to the Sierra de Francia and River Alagon.[46] The remainder of the British cavalry occupied the valley of the Mondego.[47]

On the 14th May, Mr. Charles M'Carthy became quartermaster of the regiment *vice* Jameson. Quartermaster M'Carthy was afterwards, on the 11th March 1813, promoted to be cornet, and subsequently, in May 1814, he became Lieutenant and Adjutant.

The following incidents, mentioned by General Brotherton, refer to the occasion of the retreat from Madrid, when the 14th Light Dragoons formed the rearguard of General Hill's force:—

> On our retreat from Madrid, the first day we reached a large village called Valdemoro, famous for good wine and extensive wine-vaults. *Of course* our men on arriving broke into these vaults and got drunk. The French, who were closely following us, followed their example, and found numbers of our drunken soldiers in the vaults, a large number stretched insensibly drunk. However, instead of fighting each other, they fraternised and embraced. I was sent back to this village by Lord Hill to try and get our men out of it. The scene I beheld in these vaults beggars all description, and it was, moreover, a service of danger to go amongst this motley and drunken crew of both nations, and I wonder I escaped. After almost fruitless endeavours I succeeded in bringing away but very few of these drunken brutes.
>
> A remarkable circumstance, which gave rise to much displeasure from Lord Wellington, though a trivial one, if not a *ludicrous*

---

46. The Alagon joins the Tagus above Alcantara.
47. A large portion of the narrative of the Peninsular War in this *Record* has been taken from Napier's *History* almost *verbatim*, and many details are also taken from Cannon's *Historical Record of the 14th Light Dragoons*.

one, happened on the first night of our retreat from Salamanca. The army was left *totally* without rations of any sort, and almost starving, owing to neglect in the commissariat department. The forest in which we were bivouacked abounded in large herds of pigs, amounting to many thousands—tempting objects to a starving army. Many of these droves passed along the front of our army as if saying, "Come, kill me." No wonder that volley after volley were let fly at them, laying thousands prostrate. This, of course, when so close to the enemy as we were, our vedettes almost touching each other, was a dreadful irregularity.

Lord Wellington roused out of his sleep and rode immediately to the front, thinking the enemy were attacking. His indignation on finding the cause of alarm was excessive, and the consequence was that he, next day, issued a most severe censure. The pork, I well recollect, was most delicious, hunger being the sauce, besides which these pigs feed on nothing but acorns and chestnuts, which abound in these forests. The scene in front of the line was a most extraordinary one.

As the night had been very dark when these droves of pigs rushed past the front, the men fired their volleys at random, and many in front, particularly the cavalry, suffered. I myself saw two heavy dragoons and one horse lying dead. I shall never forget the singularity of the scene at dawn of day, close to the bivouac of the 14th Light Dragoons, and near where Lord Wellington himself had bivouacked, surrounded as it was by dead pigs strewed on the ground, dead dragoons, dead horses, etc. etc.!

I went out one morning, very early, during the disastrous retreat from Salamanca to Ciudad Rodrigo, *en parlementaire*, to inquire at the French outposts as to the fate of a gallant fellow who was orderly dragoon to Colonel Hervey, who, the night before, going his rounds with this orderly, went by mistake (the night being very dark and the enemy's picquets and ours very close together) up to a French picquet, and finding his mistake galloped off; but his gallant orderly, in order to save him from his pursuers—he, Colonel Hervey, having only one arm—sacrificed himself and kept sabring with the enemy to give time to Colonel Hervey to escape, which he did, though with difficulty. The orderly did not rejoin him, and we were anxious next morning to ascertain his fate, and know whether he was dead or alive.

Accordingly, I proceeded early in the morning, accompanied by a trumpeter, towards the enemy's outposts. I found the enemy advancing, with skirmishers extended. I turned round to the trumpeter and told him to sound something to show I was a flag of truce.

He thoughtlessly sounded the "charge," upon which (it being a forest and a foggy morning) the enemy imagined we were advancing in force and precipitately retired. I kept following them to endeavour to undeceive them, and at last they halted; and when I came up to the officer he seemed rather ashamed and vexed at what had happened.

I shall never forget the *figure* he was. It was a very wet morning, and we had bivouacked without any shelter. He wore *trousers*. The French officers are not very particular about dress. To the sorrow of the whole regiment I found the gallant fellow (Sergeant Puss, a picked man) had perished in his noble struggle to save his colonel, having been cut to pieces. In reference to the above, the trumpeter with me was a German, and consequently, not attached to us by any feeling. Whilst I was talking to the French officer he galloped off towards the French lines, evidently with the intention of deserting, for the great temptation to do so was that deserters were allowed to sell the horses on which they deserted.

The French officer, a chivalrous fellow, was indignant at the infamous conduct of the trumpeter, and immediately sent one of his men in pursuit of him, to bring him back and deliver him up to me for punishment; but as I knew he must have been hanged if I took him back to camp, I declined to receive him. The German and other foreign soldiers were not to be trusted always, as they changed sides as suited their convenience, at the risk of being hanged, either by the French or ourselves.

When the 14th Light Dragoons were cantoned in Portugal in 1812 at Fundão, a large proportion of the troop-horses were turned out to grass more than five miles from the town. They had previously been groomed and fed every day at particular hours in the great square. The day after they were turned out they all came galloping in at the accustomed hour of feeding, and placed themselves in the square as if they had been led there!

1813

After passing the winter in cantonments among the Portuguese peasantry, the Fourteenth once more crossed the confines of that kingdom and formed part of the centre column of the allied army in the general advance which commenced in May. Wellington had with him 70,000 men and 90 pieces of artillery. The French Armies scattered through Spain numbered probably not more than 160,000 men altogether, but of these there were probably not more than 110,000 in the united armies opposed to Wellington. During the advance the allies were at first divided into three parts, and the Fourteenth entered Spain in the advance-guard of the centre column, arriving at Salamanca on 26th May, when the bridge and streets were found barricaded,[48] and a force under General Villates was formed on the heights above the ford of Santa Marta, consisting of a division of French infantry, 3 squadrons of cavalry, and some artillery.

A British brigade passed the river at the ford, and the Fourteenth, with the 1st German Hussars, in brigade under Major-General Baron Victor Alten, removed the barricades and pushed through the town. The enemy fell back, but was overtaken, and lost about 200 men killed and wounded, as well as 200 prisoners. The line of the Tormes was thus gained, and that of the Duero soon afterwards, so that the allied army now firmly advanced and speedily passed the Carrion and the Pisuerga.

During these movements the Fourteenth formed, as usual, part of the advance-guard of the army, and was engaged on 12th June near Burgos, where the Light Division, Grant's Hussar Brigade, and Ponsonby's Brigade of dragoons turned the French right, while the rest of the troops attacked the whole range of heights extending from Hormillas to Estepar, held by the French under Reille, who barred the way to Burgos.

Reille began to fall back for the bridge of Baniel on the Arlanzon,[49] but during this movement Gardiner's Horse Artillery raked his columns, and Captain Milles of the Fourteenth, at the head of a squadron, charged and took several prisoners and a gun. The Fourteenth lost 1 man and 1 horse killed, 1 man and 5 horses wounded. After this the French destroyed Burgos castle, and fell back with tumult and confusion behind the Ebro, the British following up towards the sources of that river, and marching through a wild and beautiful district com-

---

48. Cannon's *Record*.
49. Napier, vol. v.

pletely turned the enemy's position, cutting him entirely off from the sea-coast. On the 15th June the Fourteenth, being in advance, crossed the Ebro at the bridge of Frias, [50] and a patrol fell in with a body of the enemy near Pancorba.

The French under King Joseph and Marshal Jourdain were concentrated in front of Vittoria. Wellington had only 60,000 Anglo-Portuguese sabres and bayonets with him, the 6th Division, 6500 strong, being left at Medina de Pomar. The Spanish auxiliaries were above 20,000. The approximate number of the French was about 60,000, but in the number and size of their guns they had the advantage. The enemy had many thousand carriages and impediments of all kinds heaped about Vittoria, which blocked all the roads and created confusion among the artillery parks.[51] On the 20th June the Marquis of Wellington examined the position taken up by the French Army, and that day the Fourteenth skirmished with the enemy near the village of Huarte.

The troops under Lieutenant-General Sir Rowland Hill, amongst whom were the Fourteenth, in the Battle of Vittoria on 21st June, were told off to attack the enemy's left. They consisted of 20,000 men, composed of Morillo's Spaniards, Silveira's Portuguese, and the 2nd British Division, with cavalry and guns. The scene of the battlefield was a very rugged country on the banks of the Zadora and Bayas Rivers, and there were no less than seven bridges within the area of operations.

At daybreak on the 21st June, the weather being rainy with a thick vapour, the troops moved from their camps on the Bayas, and the centre of the army advancing in columns passed the ridges in front, and slowly approached the Zadora. The left column pointed to Mendoza, the right column skirted the Morillas ridge, on the other side of which Hill's Corps was marching, and the latter General seized the village of Puebla about 10 o'clock. Hill having crossed the mountains, where he was vigorously opposed by the enemy under Gazan and Villate, won the village of Subijana de Alava on the other side, and eventually outflanked the enemy's left late in the afternoon.

At first the Fourteenth supported the attacks of the infantry and artillery, and later in the day were detached to help in the successful turning movements on the left flank of the French. Graham led the attack on the French right, while Wellington himself, at a time when he

---

50. Cannon's *Record*.
51. Napier.

Uniform of Major-General of Light Dragoons

Lieut. Col. of 14th Light Dragoons
in parade dress

observed the French central positions somewhat denuded of troops, brought up Picton's 3rd Division against the weakened positions with crushing effect, and after a long and fiercely contested battle, which lasted till past 6 o'clock in the evening, the French Army was completely routed and driven in confusion off the field.[52] Napier says:—

> Never was a victory more complete. The trophies were innumerable. The French carried off but two pieces of artillery from the battle (and one of these was afterwards taken at Pampeluna). Jourdain's baton of command, a stand of colours, 143 brass pieces, all the parks and depots from Madrid, Valladolid, and Burgos, carriages, ammunition, treasure of enormous value everything fell into the hands of the victors.

The loss of men was about 6000 on the French side and 5000 on the side of the allies. The plunder and spoil was immense, chiefly carried off by the followers and non-combatants. In the evening the Fourteenth, serving in Victor Alten's Brigade,[53] were employed in the pursuit of the wreck of the French Army along the Pampeluna road, following the direction taken by King Joseph, who had continued his retreat up the Borundia and Avaquil valleys all night, and they passed the whole of the enemy's baggage, which had been abandoned in the flight. On the 24th they came up with the French rear-guard at a pass two leagues from Pampeluna, when the leading squadron of the regiment under Major Brotherton charged and captured a tumbril. In this pursuit the Fourteenth were supported by Colonel Ross's Light Artillery troops. The main body of the French Army now retreated into France by the valley of Roncesvalles, pursued by the British.

This Battle of Vittoria was the crowning victory of the war in the Peninsula. The actual scene of the battle was on ground quite unsuitable for cavalry movements, but the Fourteenth and other cavalry during several days afterwards took a very active part in the pursuit of the enemy right into the Pyrenees. The rain for two days following the battle was most vehement and incessant, and as the Pampeluna road was swampy and much blocked, and the fugitive enemy set fire to the villages behind them, the pursuit was necessarily very difficult. On the 28th June, Lieutenant Ward, with a patrol of 3 men of the Fourteenth, got as far as the village of Ostiz, where he found 25 French

---

52. Napier.
53. At Vittoria, Victor Alten's Brigade consisted of the 14th Light Dragoons, as well as the 1st and 2nd regiments of Hussars of the King's German Legion.

foot-soldiers regularly armed and formed up at the village, but these surrendered themselves prisoners of war. Another patrol of the Fourteenth, consisting of 6 men under Lieutenant Clavering, penetrated still further into the mountains, and encountered on the 1st July a body of infantry of the French rearguard, on the road leading from Roncesvalles to St. Jean-Pied-de-Port, in the Basses Pyrenees. This patrol dispersed the enemy and took 18 of them prisoners.

It was probably in this pursuit, commenced on the evening of the victory at Vittoria, along the Pampeluna road, that the Fourteenth earned a title to that elegant and historical piece of silver plate known as 'The Emperor,' which has so long adorned the officers' mess. It was the property of His Majesty Joseph Buonaparte, King of Spain, and the royal arms are still discernible upon it. 'The Emperor,' in the piping times of peace, is seldom seen except when filled to the brim with the choicest brands of champagne, and in this condition it has passed through successive generations of the regiment, and done duty as a loving-cup in the officers' mess on many festive occasions.

For its gallant bearing at Vittoria the Fourteenth were subsequently (in 1820) rewarded with the royal authority to bear the word 'Vittoria 'on their regimental guidons and appointments, and an additional honorary distinction was conferred on the (1820). commanding officer, Lieutenant-Colonel Sir. B. Hervey, Bart.

The following anecdotes are related by General Brotherton regarding the advance to Burgos and the Battle of Vittoria:—

On the advance of the army to Burgos we had been engaged the whole day with the enemy, and my charger was quite worn out with fatigue towards night. A few days before, I had received from England a young horse, quite unbroke and wild. The enemy having unexpectedly advanced again late in the evening, after we had retired to our camp, thinking the work quite over for that day, on the "alert" being given (my charger being too much knocked up) I jumped on the young horse, who had only a snaffle-bridle on, not thinking there would be much to do. However, we had a stiff struggle with the enemy to drive him back, in which, charging at the head of my squadron, this said young horse ran away with me, and was taking me right into the French squadron opposed to us, when at the distance of thirty or forty yards, I threw myself off, to escape being carried into the ranks of the enemy. The few men who were following me dragged me away, as I clung to their stirrups.

In the meantime my horse proceeded straight forward, and literally dashed through the centre of the French squadron, where I need not say he was secured, and proved a most acceptable acquisition, being a remarkably fine, valuable young horse. Those who were looking on on this occasion thought me most rash, not knowing I was run away with, and Lord Wellington himself was much amused when he learned the real state of the case.

Riding over the field of battle, I stopped to give a wounded French officer a drink of water, which he was piteously calling out for. He was mortally wounded, and the blood gushing out from his wound. On my speaking a few words of consolation and comfort to him he could not help, even in his agonies, expressing his indignation at King Joseph and Marshal Jourdain, the general commanding. He said their army was more *un bordel ambulant* than a fighting army.

And indeed it was a strange scene. The plunder of years collected, hordes of the Spanish women who had been seduced by the French officers and men, and lastly, King Joseph's own seraglio of courtly ladies, cooped up in carriages of which we had taken possession, forming a procession nearly a mile long; the carriages ransacked by our soldiery, and every valuable taken out of them, but a bottle of brandy seized by them more eagerly than precious jewels.

I had collected a considerable quantity of plate, plunder at the Battle of Vittoria, which I purchased at the auctions of it that took place in the different corps. When I was taken prisoner all this was sold along with my other effects, as it is the custom in the British service.

I never could get back any part of this plate, though I had applied to those who had purchased it and offered a high value for it, wishing to preserve it as a memorial of the battle. Amongst others, a Captain —— of my own regiment had purchased a coffee-pot, and I offered him the choice of London for a similar article, if he would return it to me, but he would not. I call this *churlish*, particularly in a brother officer.

Talking of plate, I will just mention an anecdote showing that there is "*nothing new under the sun*," and that *fashion* in plate, as well as in everything else, constantly revolves and returns to old things again. I purchased of an old Spaniard, whose ancestors had resided in South America, some silver spoons made in that country more than *a hundred years ago*, of exactly the fashion and make of the present day.

The result of the Battle of Vittoria was a total rout of the French Army, and the capture of all their baggage, artillery, etc. etc. The rich plunder was to an enormous extent, but the troops (that is the "combatants"), however, profited comparatively but little, as they were too busily employed in following the enemy, and could not stop to plunder, so that all valuables fell to the share of the "non-combatants" and civilians attached to the army. Amongst the former may be classed the farriers of the cavalry, who are never in the ranks, and who frequently stop behind to plunder the wounded and the dead under pretence of shoeing horses. On this occasion our farriers of the Fourteenth took advantage of this trick to stop behind and plunder the very carriages which the regiment had passed and not touched: such was the severity of discipline in such cases, that not a single man dismounted to touch anything.

Not so the farriers who lingered behind. They all carried what are called "churns," *viz*. large leather cases placed where the dragoon's holsters for his pistols are placed, and these they crammed with the abundant spoil of jewellery, etc., which they got by handfuls out of the carriages; and moreover, they had overtaken some mules belonging to the Pay Department of the French army, but abandoned by those who led them, carrying large boxes of dollars and other monies.

When we arrived at the end of our pursuit of the routed French Army, which terminated at Pampeluna, Colonel Hervey, who was aware of the immense booty in possession of the farriers, who, as "non-combatants," were far less entitled to it than their comrades in the ranks, who had fought hard for it, and who had first come up to it, but were restrained from plundering by their exemplary discipline, [Colonel Hervey] in order to pounce upon the plunder of these farriers, who, he knew, had not had time to dispose of it, suddenly ordered the "Rouse and Assembly" to be sounded in the camp, and the whole regiment being assembled, farriers and all (these little suspecting the object of the sudden parade), he ordered a square to be formed, brought all the farriers to the middle of it, dismounted them, had their

---

54. Val de Bastan, in Navarre.

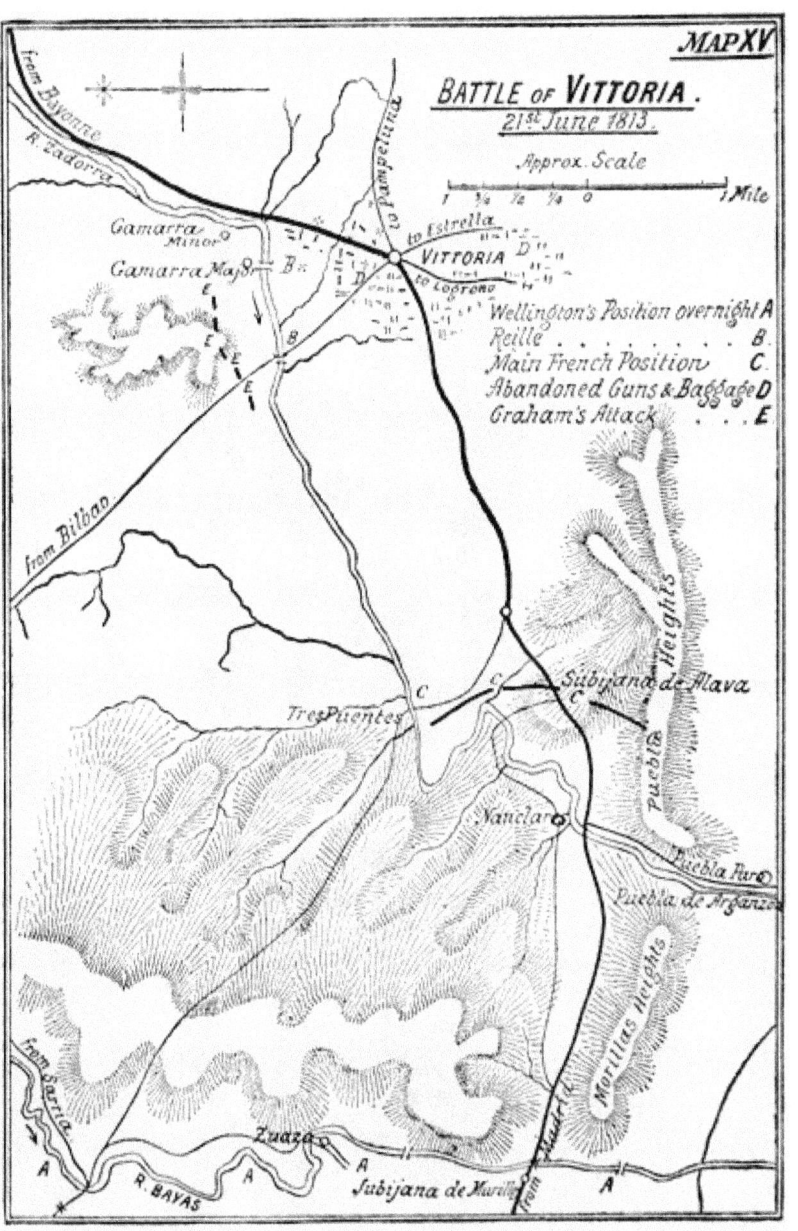

churns taken off, and the plunder disgorged from them, to the joy and glee of the whole corps, who were justly entitled to it. I shall never forget the scene! There was perhaps more valuable plunder at Vittoria than at any other battle of modern times.

The French Army was dragging after it, as it was evacuating Spain, the accumulation of the plunder and robbery of *years*, during the whole time of their occupation of the country. The civilians of the army, *viz.* the commissariat, storekeepers, and paymasters, made enormously. One commissary got hold of a chest of gold *doubloons*, said to amount to £10,000. He thought he would secure it by throwing it (for the time), unperceived, as he imagined, in a deep river, the Zadora, which ran through the field of battle, but he had been observed by some Spanish muleteers, who reported the circumstance. The box was fished up, and the contents credited to the legitimate captors, *viz.* the army at large.

An intimate friend in the infantry had often made me promise that, if ever he was so severely wounded as to require amputation of a limb, and he happened to be in too weak a state to resist the operation, I would not allow it to be performed, as he said he would rather die than undergo the operation. He was shot through both legs, on the advance to Vittoria, and immediately sent for me, and earnestly reminded me of my promise, as the surgeons insisted on amputating in spite of his remonstrances, and he felt too weak to offer resistance.

It was an awkward position, I having solemnly promised to interfere, but the surgeons assured me that he must die if the operations were delayed. The poor fellow, whose name was Burgess, looked at me pitifully and reproachfully, as he saw that I felt disinclined to fulfil my promise. Whilst this painful scene was going on a sudden bleeding came on, and he died in my arms.

Soon after the Battle of Vittoria, King Joseph had sent a strong body of French troops into Spain again, to hold the valley of Bastan in the Pyrenees,[54] which was a very fertile spot and also full of strong military positions. Lieutenant-General Sir Rowland Hill's Division, consisting of 2 brigades of British and 2 brigades of Portuguese troops, was at once marched there to endeavour to drive out the French. The Fourteenth were attached to this division, and during the four

Napoleon's chamber-pot taken at Vittoria

days from 4th to 7th July vigorous movements took place, in which the troops under Lieutenant-General Sir Rowland Hill succeeded in driving the enemy from all the positions occupied without incurring much loss themselves. The Fourteenth took an active part in these operations, and on 4th July, Major Brotherton, with a squadron of the regiment, had an encounter with the French near Almandoz.

By this time the allies had established themselves in mountain positions along the edge of the Pyrenees, and occupied the whole line of the Spanish frontier from Roncesvalles to the mouth of the River Bidassoa. They had also invested the towns of Pampeluna and St. Sebastian. King Joseph's reign had practically ceased after the battle of Vittoria, the day of humiliation for France, and the downfall of Napoleon was drawing near. The Fourteenth took the outpost duties in front of Maya, a pass of the Pyrenees, and furnished posts of correspondence during several weeks.

After a while the French Army was reinforced and reorganised, and Marshal Soult took the supreme command, and advanced to oppose the allies. Important actions were fought on the 25th and 26th July near the Maya Pass, and the allies were forced to retire. On the 26th the Fourteenth were employed in carrying off the wounded from the field during the action, and were publicly thanked by Lieutenant-General Sir Rowland Hill for the efficient manner in which this duty was performed.

On 30th July, when the post at Arestegui was attacked and an action took place, Major Brotherton's squadron of the Fourteenth was engaged, and Captain Milles's squadron was employed in carrying off the wounded from the field. In August the Fourteenth, forming the van of Lieutenant-General Sir Rowland Hill's Division, were engaged with the enemy in the valley of Bastan, in Navarre. Fighting took place on the 1st and 2nd of August, when the French were repulsed. On 5th August the regiment again took the outpost duty in front of Maya.

The siege of San Sebastian, the blockade of Pampeluna, and other sieges and military operations on the confines of Spain and in the Pyrenees occupied a large portion of the allied army for the next two months. On the 8th October, Wellington's army crossed the river Bidassoa and entered French territory. During the same month headquarters were fixed in Vera, and the army was organised in three grand divisions. [55] The right was commanded by Lieutenant-General

---
55. Napier.

Sir R. Hill, and extended from Roncesvalles to the Bastan; the centre column, occupying Maya, the Echallar, Rhune, and Bayonettes mountains, was under Lieutenant-General Beresford; [56] and the left, extending from the Mandale mountain to the sea, was under General Sir John Hope. [57]

By the end of October the troops in the mountain passes above Roncesvalles were knee-deep in snow, provisions were scanty, and the privations of the allies were greater even than those of the French army under Marshal Soult on the opposite side of the Pyrenees. Finer weather set in on 6th and 7th November, and Wellington determined to advance into France, but on the 8th heavy rain caused a postponement of the forward movement. On the 10th November the troops descended the Pyrenees, traversing the mountain passes by moonlight, where they halted when they reached the line of picquets, and at daybreak crossed into France.

The Fourteenth were attached to Lieutenant-General Sir Rowland Hill's Division, and one squadron of the regiment formed Marshal Beresford's advance-guard. The enemy's position on the Nivelle was forced, and on the following day the regiment was united at Espelette. The regimental baggage, which was attached to the 2nd Division, fell into the hands of the enemy in the rear of the pass of Maya, and on that occasion 1 troop sergeant-major and 2 privates of the Fourteenth were killed. [58]

The Fourteenth lost their regimental documents and papers in charge of the paymaster and adjutant, as well as the officers' personal baggage. The escort made a very gallant defence under a staff officer who was in charge on this occasion. The loss of these official documents belonging to the Fourteenth was a very serious matter for the regiment, and probably many interesting and valuable records which could not be replaced disappeared on this occasion. General Brotherton relates as follows concerning the incident:—

> Never form a hasty opinion of any man's courage in the field! In a tried corps, such as the 14th Light Dragoons was towards the close of the Peninsular War, we knew each other pretty well, and our comparative value, individually, in the field, both officers and men; but still prejudices were entertained against certain individuals who, if not absolutely shy in action, were

---
56. Afterwards General Viscount Beresford, G.C.B., G.C.H.
57. Afterwards General Lord Niddry, and later Earl of Hopetoun, G.C.B.
58. Cannon's *Record*.

An officer of Light Dragoons in review dress

considered not very forward, to say the least of it. One of the most remarkable instances of the sort that occurred, in which the judgment proved erroneous and unjust, was that of a troop-sergeant-major, a *nervous* man only, of no great reputation in the field, and who on that account was usually selected to assist in the command of the baggage, which generally followed at some distance in the rear of the regiment.

On one occasion, however, the last on which the poor fellow saw an enemy, the baggage was surprised, and all taken. It was in the Pyrenees, on the first day of our descent into France, 10th November 1813, a brilliant day for the British arms. Our baggage went astray, and got separated from us by one of those deep, narrow precipices so frequent in these mountains, and we had the mortification of seeing our baggage assailed immediately under our own eyes, and almost within carbine range, by a battalion of French "*voltigeurs*," who took the whole of it, but not till after a *desperate resistance* on the part of the baggage-guard under the command of Sergeant-Major B——, whom we distinctly saw most bravely distinguishing himself to save the baggage, till he and most of the guard fell.

We witnessed this tardy but brilliant justification of his character with mixed emotions of admiration, but deep regret at having so long done him an injustice. It was a lesson that ought never to be forgotten, and should teach all soldiers to be charitable, and not hasty in their judgments upon their comrades in the field.

From the 15th of November to the 9th of December the Fourteenth furnished the outposts on the River Nive,[59] and formed the advance-guard to Sir Rowland Hill's Corps at the passage of that river, which was effected at the fords of Cambo, where the stream being deep, 2 men and 2 horses belonging to the regiment were unfortunately drowned.

On 11th December a squadron of the Fourteenth under command of Major Brotherton was engaged with a body of the enemy near Mendionda, and captured a convoy of corn, wine, and salt, making 4 men as well as 4 horses of the escort prisoners.

On 13th December, at Hasparren in the Basses Pyrénées, the Four-

---

59. The 13th and 14th Light Dragoons were engaged in the operations by which the passage of the Nive was effected on the 9th December 1813.—Cannon's *Historical Record of the 13th Light Dragoons*.

teenth as well as part of the 13th Light Dragoons were engaged with the French light cavalry commanded by General Pièrre Soult (brother of the marshal), and on this occasion Major Brotherton, 1 sergeant, and 1 private were wounded, and Lieutenant the Honourable H. Southwell's horse was killed. Major Brotherton, Lieutenant the Honourable H. Southwell, and 1 man were taken prisoners by the enemy. The Fourteenth drove the enemy out of Hasparren. Referring to the affair at Hasparren and the forcing of the Nive on the 9th December, the following incidents are related by General Brotherton:—

> The most guarded and considerate judgment should ever be passed on the deportment of soldiers in the field, young or old, as the following anecdote will show:—
> General Sir —— was known in the army as a gallant soldier, and though somewhat slow, and not brilliant in action, yet he had always done his duty. On the 9th December 1813, the day on which we forced the passage of the River Nive, in the south of France, at the bridge of Cambo, Sir ——'s brigade being in line, but lying down as the enemy were throwing shot and shells at it, the general, also sitting down in front, surrounded by his staff, and taking the opportunity of eating a mouthful, and drinking a glass of wine before commencing the attack he beckoned me to partake of his grog, which I willingly did, having eaten nothing since noon on the preceding day. I squatted myself down with the party.
> The enemy's fire was doing but little mischief; still, it was necessary to keep out of sight as much as possible, in order not to attract more fire. However, just as we were filling our mouths, and helping ourselves to a glass of wine, a shell came over us, and fell within four or five yards of our group, but buried itself so deeply in the ground that it was easy, with the least presence of mind, to see that its explosion would be harmless, or nearly so. The general had his glass of wine up to his mouth at the very moment the shell fell; he instantly threw away his glass of wine on the ground, and himself *flat on his belly*, which is the usual mode resorted to in order to escape the effect of the explosion of a shell, which, when it bursts, cannot hurt you when you are in this position. *We*, the group round the general, could not help roaring with laughter at the risible operation the general had gone through from his nervousness, and indeed the whole

brigade, lying down in line, roared with laughter also at their general's ridiculous predicament, sprawling on the ground. A poor young fellow, his *aide-de-camp*, young of the 3rd Guards, who joined heartily in the joke, was shortly afterwards killed, on another occasion.

I relate this anecdote, not in disparagement of, or with any disrespect towards General ——, and his reputation can well bear that such an anecdote be told of him, but only to show the occasional *nervousness* which the best seasoned soldier (and General —— had been a great deal under fire during a long military career) will sometimes involuntarily betray under fire.

'Had this happened to a young untried soldier, he would have felt ashamed of himself perhaps, though without reason, for his moral courage to do his duty might be equal to any man's, notwithstanding his physical nerves failed him in this way.

One of the bravest men of his day, L'Amiral Coligni, in Henri Quatre's time, used to say, "*On nest pas brave étgalement tous les jours*" and no doubt this is perfectly true. One's nerves are not equally strong every day. Let us therefore put the most favourable and charitable construction on the deportment of men in battle, till we find out they are really good for nothing.

The night before the battle (for the 13th December 1813 *was* a battle, and a sanguinary one too), as the Duke of Wellington had promised me a step of rank on the first occasion it could be granted—and I was then only a major—Sir Hussey Vivian, who was the general commanding our brigade, being a great friend of mine, and anxious to afford me an opportunity of distinguishing myself, arranged that I should lead the charge (a sort of forlorn hope) with a certain number of picked men, to drive the enemy out of the village of Hasparren, which they occupied in force. Accordingly, early in the morning of the 13th, I descended towards the village with my party, immediately supported by a half squadron, and found the enemy, the 13th Chasseurs, and Chamboran (2nd) Hussars, posted behind a narrow bridge, at the entrance of the village.

I immediately ordered the trumpeter to sound the "charge," so that those behind us who were to support should advance at the same time, and putting myself at the head of my men, rode at the enemy; but as the bridge was a very narrow one, only myself, Lieutenant Southwell (a distinguished officer, whom I had chosen to accompany me), and my orderly, could pass over at a time, which we accordingly did. The enemy received us with a volley from their pistols and carbines, when we were close upon them. Southwell's horse fell dead, and he fell under him.

However, myself and orderly closed with the enemy. The orderly had his bridle-hand nearly chopped off, and was run through the body, and I was then left alone amidst the enemy. I was belaboured with cuts and thrusts from all sides, defending myself as long as I could against such odds. However, after receiving eleven thrusts, *three* of which *only* wounded me (as I wore a buffalo leather *cuirass* which I had made at Madrid, after having been run through the body at Salamanca), I was wounded through the neck, in the right hip, or to speak more plainly, in the bottom, on the right side, and another stab in the thigh, which would have proved the worst of all, had it not been for a bunch of letters which I had that morning received from England, and which I had put into one of the pockets which were then worn with pantaloons.

The sword penetrated the letters, and went a quarter of an inch into the thigh, close to what is called, I believe, the femoral artery, which, had it touched, probably it would have proved fatal; but the blow which rendered it impossible to make further resistance was a sabre-cut, aimed at my head, which fell on the peak of my helmet with such force that it bent it on my nose, which it flattened and nearly broke, and completely stunned me. As I said, this blow disabled me from further resistance, and, indeed, no signs of any assistance appearing, rendered it useless to resist any longer.

Surrounded as I was by fellows cutting and thrusting at me in all directions, and so occupied was I in parrying, that I had not time for assaulting in my turn. It was my intention to surrender, but a little circumstance caused me to be much more roughly treated than I otherwise should probably have been.

I had, previously to advancing to the "charge," twisted my silk sword-knot round and round my wrist, by way of securing my sword the more effectually; and when stunned by the cut on my helmet, which I have just before mentioned, and summoned on all sides by vociferations to surrender (*rendez vous*), my sword was seized, but as it was so tightly fastened to my wrist, this was taken for an intention not to surrender it; and a fellow cocked his pistol, and put it to my head to blow out my brains, when I had just sufficiently recovered to articulate *Je me rends!*

I was then secured, and tied on my horse, being too faint to sit on it otherwise, and galloped off to the rear (like Mazeppa), for by this time Sir Hussey Vivian and his whole brigade were advancing to rescue me. The mare I rode (the same as was wounded near Salamanca) got her head cut open on this occasion, but behaved most gallantly. She reared and literally *pawed*, when on her hind legs, at my antagonists. I will add a little anecdote that happened when the French surgeon was dressing the wound in my neck, as it is to his credit, and shows that chivalrous spirit with which war was then carried on:—

I always wore eight or ten gold pieces, of about £3 each, in a piece of black silk, round my neck, in case of need, if taken prisoner. I had wore this so long, that the silk was a good deal worn out, and showed the gold. On taking off my stock to look at the wound, the surgeon, perceiving this, immediately covered my neck again, and whispered to me (for the French Hussars who had brought me to the rear were looking on) that I had better conceal the money. I desired him, however, to take it and give it to the men, whose lawful prize it was.

I tried to recover my mare, and offered any sum to get her and send her back, but in vain, for she was evidently of the purest Arabian breed: she was sent to one of the Imperial studs. My exchange for a French officer of equal rank was arranged, the very day after I was taken, and he was sent over to his army; but through the bad faith of Marshal Soult, I was detained under the pretence, at first, that wounds disabled me from being sent, but, as I found out afterwards, through an idea that I had seen so much of the country, through which our army was likely to advance, as to be enabled to give information disadvantageous to the enemy.

When taken prisoner on the 13th December 1813, and taken to the rear of the French Army, and smarting and lame with my wounds, on one of the day's halts I stopped at Tarbes. This is a town famous for cutlery, and I had a *billet de logement* (the troops in France being always quartered in private houses) at a rich cutler's who, not expecting, I suppose, the further advance of the British Army, and the occupation of Tarbes by British troops, was extremely brutal and unkind to me, which, in my helpless state, I felt most keenly, but was soon revenged on the brute, for, one morning early, that I was sent off further to the rear, on the report that the British Army was advancing, "mine host" came to me in a most sneaking humble way, very different from the insolent one he had hitherto behaved to me, and asked me for a letter that might be some sort of protection to his person and property on the entrance of the British troops into Tarbes. I thought it an excellent opportunity of "paying him off," as the saying is, and, as he did not understand a word of English (and very few people in this part of France do), I wrote a "protecting pass" for this scoundrel as follows:—

> The bearer of this is one of the greatest brutes that ever breathed. He treated me like a dog during the time I was lying wounded in his house, and I strongly recommend him to the special notice of all British soldiers, who, no doubt, will treat him as he deserves, for his infamous treatment of their wounded comrade.

By a strange fatality it so happened that it was a party of my own regiment, the 14th Light Dragoons, that formed the advance-guard of the British army and first entered Tarbes, and to whom the cutler presented my certificate. I need not say that he was "paid off." They nearly killed him!

When I was taken prisoner on 13th December 1813, I was a major in the 14th Light Dragoons, and was promised my rank of lieutenant-colonel on the first battle. I was given a sort of "forlorn hope" to give me an opportunity of distinguishing myself. I was severely wounded, and if I did not succeed it was not my fault. Being a prisoner, however, I was left out of the brevet that was given for the battle.

This was a hard case, though it is the custom of the service. I never recovered the ground I lost by this disappointment.

The charger I rode during most of the Peninsular War was the one I rode when taken prisoner, as related above. She was bought by my father (who was a great judge of horses) at the sale of the King's stud, at three years old. She was of the purest Arabian blood, and perfect symmetry, fifteen hands high, dark brown, a perfect picture, most graceful in all her movements, but very conceited. As she walked along she looked to the right and to the left, as if to see who was admiring her. She was the admiration of the whole army. She was so sagacious that marvellous stories were told of her. She always wore a silken net to protect her from the flies that maddened her when she hadn't it on.

She was wounded several times. At Salamanca a shell shattered her stifle or thigh, and I was nearly advised to shoot her as incurable, but the stud groom of Lord Charles Manners effected a perfect cure after a long time, only leaving an immense scar and dent.

She was twice wounded by sabre-cuts on the head. The last time was in the *mêlée* on December 13, 1813, when I was taken prisoner, when she actually reared and pawed my antagonist, as if to defend me. She had her head cut open in a dreadful way. Still, I offered any sum to purchase her, but she became the property of the French Government, and was sent to a breeding stud, where her pure blood was most valuable. I was often tempted, by large offers, to sell her. Sir Charles Stewart, since Lord Londonderry, had offered me 300 guineas for her.

She was, though of excellent temper, difficult to ride, from her fiery disposition. In bivouac, when lying down beside me, she would lift up her head to see if I was sleeping, and if she saw I was she would immediately lie down again, for fear of disturbing me. She was particularly fond of raw beef-steaks, and it was difficult to keep the men's rations from her, even if suspended on trees as they usually were, by way of safety. Her name was "Fatima."

After the victory of St. Pierre, near Bayonne, on 13th December, Wellington was firmly established on the Adour. On the 14th December the Fourteenth took the outpost duty in front of Urt, near the River Adour, and on 21st December parties from both the 13th and 14th Light Dragoons shared the outpost work at Urcuit and La Bastide, both the latter places being somewhat to the south of Urt. The two regiments (13th and 14th Light Dragoons), known as the 'Ragged Brigade,' were now under Brigadier-General Vivian (afterwards Sir Hussey Vivian), and he was succeeded in the beginning of 1814 by Major-General Fane. [60] The army under Lord Wellington now took a

---

60. During the Peninsular War the Fourteenth served in brigades at various times under the following officers as brigadiers, *viz*:—1809, Cotton; 1810-11, Slade; 1811, Arentschild; 1812-13, Victor Alten; 1813, Long, Grant, and Vivian; 1814, Fane and Doherty.

short rest in quarters during very severe and inclement weather before resuming work again in the middle of February.

After the Battle of Vittoria and the pursuit to Pampeluna the Fourteenth were brigaded with the 13th Light Dragoons, when they were nicknamed the 'Ragged Brigade,' first under the command of Major-General Long, then in November 1813 under Brigadier-General Grant, and subsequently under Brigadier-General Richard Hussey Vivian (afterwards Major-General Sir Hussey Vivian, K.C.B.), during the advance into France, and in 1814 under Major-General Sir Henry Fane, K.C.B., who commanded the brigade at the battles of Orthes, Aire, and Toulouse. The origin of the *sobriquet* of 'Ragged Brigade 'was owing to the ragged state to which those two famous fighting regiments were reduced as a result of their long-continued service in the field, and their frequent marches, bivouacs, and exposure in all weathers. [61]

It is a curious coincidence that both these regiments, who became such firm friends when on service in the Peninsula and afterwards in peace time, should have had an early history very similar one to the other. Both regiments went through those extraordinarily lengthened periods of consecutive service in Ireland during the eighteenth century, of twenty-five years at one time, and of forty-eight years at another; both regiments were engaged in the Jacobite rebellions of 1715 and 1745; in the latter year both regiments were brigaded together at Corstorphine, Coltbridge, and Haddington, under Colonel Gardiner of the Thirteenth, which regiment was then called 'Gardiner's Dragoons,' and the Fourteenth were called 'Hamilton's Dragoons,' Colonel Archibald Hamilton being their colonel. At Prestonpans the two regiments fought together, on which occasion their experiences were very similar.

In 1795 they met once more at Bristol, both being without horses, when preparing to go on service in the West Indies, where both regiments were subsequently employed in that disastrous campaign—which reduced them to skeletons by yellow fever, and from which they returned home in very reduced numbers when the operations were over. The next recorded meeting of the two regiments was in the Peninsular War, when they were christened the 'Ragged Brigade,' in 1813-14, and their next two meetings were in 1841 and 1897.

The 13th Hussars have in their possession a manuscript journal written by an officer in that regiment at the time of the Peninsular

---
61. Cannon's *Historical Record of the 13th Light Dragoons.*

War, and the following extracts, taken from that journal, were kindly given to the writer of these records by an officer of the 13th Hussars,[62] as they contain so many allusions to the doings of the Fourteenth in 1813-14, when brigaded with the Thirteenth.

Extracts from Manuscript Journal in Possession of 13th Hussars (1897)

On 9th November 1813, at Elizondo, in the Bastan Valley, Navarre, the 13th Light Dragoons were in brigade with the 14th Light Dragoons, Colonel Grant commanding the brigade in place of Colonel Long, who had been appointed to a command in England, and the two regiments marched together through the Pyrenees by the Maya Pass, thence to Urdache,[63] near the River Bidassoa, which divides France from Spain, and having crossed that river, entered French territory early on the morning of the 10th November. Here, at 3 a.m., they bivouacked after a tedious night-march across the mountains of nearly six leagues.

After a few hours' rest the brigade mounted, and advanced with the infantry, one squadron of the 14th Light Dragoons forming an advance-guard for Marshal Beresford's Corps, but the brigade really belonged to Lieutenant-General Sir Rowland Hill's Division. In a short time the advanced posts of the enemy became visible; these were all driven in, and our army came in view of the very strongly entrenched position held by the French under Marshal Soult, on the Nivelle.

This was defended by numberless redoubts bristling with cannon, and was considered impregnable—so much so that the French had erected huts in which they imagined they might securely pass the winter and bid defiance to the British advance. As the nature of the country was not suited for cavalry operations, the brigade could only witness the gallant and determined conduct of the infantry, by whom, though exposed to cannon-shot, position after position, hill after hill, forts and redoubts, were successively attacked and carried in the face of Soult's entire force, which, covering the hills on every side, lined the entrenchments, and manned the forts. The attacks were generally made at the point of the bayonet, and ultimately the enemy

---

62. Captain J. H. Tremayne (Adjt.), 13th Hussars.
63. Probably Urdax on the Nivelle, opposite to the heights of Ainhoa (Basses Pyrénées).

broke and fled in all directions, pursued by our infantry, and supported by Grant's cavalry brigade, which could only move along the roads, and even there the enemy had placed felled trees and other impediments which prevented our men from acting with effect. Towards evening the brigade retired and bivouacked in a wood, after marching about four leagues.

During the operations of this day the Spaniards had been posted on the extreme right of the British line, where they were attacked and repulsed by the enemy, in consequence of which a very large quantity of baggage belonging to the British, including that attached to the 2nd Division, which on the previous night had come safely through the Maya Pass, fell into the enemy's hands when approaching Espelette (Basses Pyrénées), and on this occasion the 14th Light Dragoons unfortunately lost their baggage, as well as a troop-sergeant-major and two privates who were killed.

On 11th November the brigade marched onwards. Putting up at the town of Arrina,[64] they moved forward again in the evening, and bivouacked near Espelette, after proceeding about three and a half leagues. On 12th and 13th November they shifted their ground and bivouacked in front of Espelette, at an advanced post two leagues to the front.

On 13th a sharp cannonade and musketry firing took place between the British, aided by the Portuguese troops, and the enemy, on the banks of the Nive, near Cambo. After dark our infantry fell back, and a frightful storm of rain, which baffles all description, continued the whole night. From 15th November to 9th December the brigade was employed in furnishing the outposts on the River Nive.

On 9th December the brigade turned out about 2 a.m., got into the positions ordered on the banks of the Nive, with the 14th Light Dragoons forming the advance-guard to the forces under Lieutenant-General Sir Rowland Hill, and by daylight a general attack commenced. The river, which was deep and strongly defended by the enemy, was forded at various points in front of our line, and the enemy was forced back on all sides. Our brigade forded the Nive, forming up on the opposite banks: the Fourteenth lost two men and two horses drowned in the deep stream of the river near Cambo. The main body of

---

64. Perhaps Ainhoûe is intended.

the infantry crossed the Nive by a bridge, formed on the opposite bank, advanced, and drove the French from every position occupied. Owing to the enclosed and hilly nature of the country the cavalry could not be brought to act with effect, so our brigade merely moved on in support of the infantry. Our brigade continued to take the outpost duties, and Brigadier-General Hussey Vivian (afterwards General Lord Vivian, G.C.B., G.C.H.) had succeeded Brigadier Grant in command. On 21st December the brigade was at Urcuit and La Bastide, somewhat to the south of Urt.

1814

In January 1814 our brigade was under the command of Major-General Fane, and a movement was made up to the high ground two leagues in front of Briscous, but the outposts there were attacked and driven in, and the ground retaken, on the 3rd January. The weather continued exceptionally severe at this season, particularly so on the 4th and 5th January, when the brigade was literally bivouacked in mud; the horses, as they stood, were covered with mud almost up to their hocks and knees. Forage had to be procured from near the enemy, and force used to obtain it.

Food also was very scarce, the usual supply being a little biscuit with spirits and water; the rain was soaking, and no baggage had come up when the brigade bivouacked on the night of the 5th January, on which day His Grace the Duke of Wellington passed by and saw for himself the state of affairs. On the 6th we moved our ground in the morning and took up a better position, and that evening Lieutenant-General the Honourable Sir Lowry Cole's and Lieutenant-General Sir Thomas Picton's Divisions came up, having been much delayed by the flooded state of the country and the incessant rains.

On 7th January the 13th Light Dragoons proceeded to Briscous and the Fourteenth to Urt, about four miles further to the north. Both regiments now reposed for a short time in these quarters, where the weather continued very severe, forage for the horses very scarce and exceedingly difficult to obtain. The usual food procurable for our horses was furze, cut and pounded and made into a sort of paste.

In February military operations were recommenced, the 14th

Light Dragoons taking the van in the advance against the enemy's left flank, which led to the subsequent actions fought at Hellette, Garris, and Sauveterre.

On 11th February the brigade moved its quarters, the Thirteenth to St. Pée and thence to Urcuray; the Fourteenth going a different route, but rejoining the 13th Light Dragoons on 13th February at a point on the St. Palais road.

On the 15th February the brigade continued its march in rear of the infantry columns, this district of the Basses Pyrénées proving quite impracticable for cavalry movements; but the infantry drove the enemy from every position occupied, and this notwithstanding the clever tactics displayed by Soult, who disputed the ground inch by inch.

At length, towards evening, it was ascertained that the French had halted, and were in position on three mountains to our front in considerable force, so our army halted and hasty dispositions were made for attack. Before the brigades had reached their several points of impact, darkness had begun to set in, but, notwithstanding this, and also that the mountain sides and their summits were crowded with the enemy's troops, nothing could resist our attack; the French were driven at every point, whilst the cheering "huzzas!" which soon rose on all sides, reverberating from mountain to mountain, proclaimed the British victory. The contest was not over till long after dark, and the enemy fought with desperation. These heights being over the town of Garris, the action goes by that name; it is near St. Palais (Basses Pyrénées).

On 16th February the brigade marched and crossed the ground where the attack had taken place the night previously; the ground was literally filled with dead. The Thirteenth were ordered to put up at St. Palais, but this town was found to be so crowded with Spaniards that it was preferred to bivouac in a wood close by, and the Fourteenth remained at Garris.

On 17th February the Thirteenth were ordered to protect the artillery and infantry and continued in front; the country was clear and open and the enemy was soon descried in view, strong in numbers, particularly in cavalry. The brigade with horse artillery was hurried to the front, and shortly afterwards the guns unlimbered and came into action; the enemy replied, and a smart cannonade ensued, to which our brigade was for some time much exposed.

The infantry eventually came up and formed to attack a village in front, on the opposite side of the river (Gave d'Oleron), and as the bridge had been destroyed by the French, His Majesty's 92nd Regiment, supported by other British troops, dashed into the water and got safely over to the opposite bank, where they re-formed and rushed forward to the attack. The enemy was now driven out of the village and pursued towards the town of Sauveterre. The infantry, with great gallantry, drove the enemy before them until he took shelter under his own guns, when our line of outposts was established, and after dark the brigade bivouacked.

On 18th February we took up a position near the village, and on 19th marched to Nabas.[65] On 20th, owing to the Spaniards having fallen back, our outposts were also thrown back.

On 21st February a reconnaissance in force was led by Lieutenant-General Sir Rowland Hill in the direction of Navarrenx. On 24th, after crossing the Gave d'Oleron at Villenave, Captain Townsend, 14th Light Dragoons, with a detachment of his regiment, encountered a body of French cavalry and took an officer prisoner, and brought him into the brigade at our bivouac that evening, when both regiments were together. The outpost duties to the right flank were taken by the Thirteenth, those to the left flank by the Fourteenth. A severe frost set in, and forage-parties were sent out after dark, but scanty supplies were obtained.

On next day (25th February) we marched to the heights above the town of Orthes, by which flows the Gave de Pau. On 26th the brigade was ready on its alarm-post, momentarily expecting to be called into action.

On 27th February the Battle of Orthes was fought. Our brigade was with Lieutenant-General Sir Rowland Hill's Corps. The 14th Light Dragoons operated against the enemy's left, after passing the stream above Orthes and advancing towards the great road leading to St. Sever, but subsequently the two regiments received orders to fall back as the French had brought artillery fire to bear from the opposite heights, and their shell and shot came amongst the brigade and through the ranks, wounding several men and horses. The fighting continued till

---

65. On the Gave de Mauleon.

dark, by which time the enemy had been forced at every point, and our victory was as complete as at Vittoria. The losses of the French are computed at from 8000 to 10,000 men in killed and wounded. Our army rested on the field, where the brigade bivouacked.

On 28th February, at daybreak, the brigade mounted, and with the horse artillery marched in pursuit through the town of Cadoures, thence six leagues onwards, taking a number of prisoners from the enemy who were retreating in disorder.

On 1st March the brigade reached the banks of the Adour, and the 14th Light Dragoons, forming the advance-guard of Lieutenant-General Sir R. Hill's Corps, forded the river, followed by the rest of the troops; but when they had advanced a league orders for our brigade to counter-march were given, and we were told to recross the river and put up wherever we could find cover, and to send out two squadrons on outpost duty under command of the field-officer of the day.

After a march of five leagues, during which the rain had fallen incessantly, the brigade found a resting-place just before dark. Before daybreak on 2nd March we assembled in brigade, and received orders to advance in front of the infantry towards Aire in Landes.

The usual advance-guard of one squadron furnished by the 14th Light Dragoons was thrown out, and it was soon reported that the greater part of the enemy were not *in* the town of Aire, but were posted in force at a point on this side of it. Lieutenant-General Sir R. Hill at once reconnoitred their position, and as the country was not suitable for cavalry operations, he immediately ordered up the infantry and made the necessary dispositions for attack. The action was completely successful, the enemy was driven from every position occupied, and ultimately from the town of Aire.

A violent and incessant rain fell with but little interruption all day and night. On the 3rd March the rain still continued to fall, accompanied by sleet and snow, but we advanced in the face of the elements, though by slow degrees, as there was also an enemy in great force, close at hand. We reached the Commune Lagos on 3rd March. On 7th March we were at Garlin: here the enemy, advancing from Conches, endeavoured, but without effect, to turn our flank.

On the 8th March we were visited on our outposts by Lieutenant-General Sir R. Hill, who ordered up three companies of the 57th Regiment to support us. On the 10th we advanced from Garlin to Tadusse, which post was very far advanced and contiguous to the enemy's lines. On the 12th we reached the great high-road leading from Conches to Lembege, where the enemy's cavalry, 800 strong, were discovered by our advanced squadron, and our brigade was retired again to Tadusse. On 13th March the enemy advanced, in considerable force of all arms, along the Lembege-Conches road.

Several encounters took place between the advanced parties of our brigade and those of the enemy. The Spanish infantry came up, but they were powerless against the superior forces of the French, and we had to fall back almost to Garlin on 14th March.

At last the British infantry arrived, and the 28th Regiment quickly drove off the enemy's sharpshooters and their supporting battalion. More British regiments came up and the enemy retreated, and our troops took possession of the heights which commanded Conches. On this day (14th March) the 14th Light Dragoons were engaged with the enemy in two affairs on the Pau road, in which they behaved with their usual bravery; in one of them Captain Babington was wounded and taken prisoner, and a few days before this Captain Townsend had been taken prisoner near Pau.

On 15th March the two regiments of the "Ragged Brigade" (13th and 14th Light Dragoons), under command of Major-General Fane, turned out and proceeded to the alarm-post on the Pau road, by daylight. Here they remained exposed to severe storms of rain and snow till between 3 and 4 o'clock p.m., when they returned to quarters. On the 16th March the two regiments again assembled at daylight at the alarm-post on the Pau road, and remained again till evening exposed to the most inclement weather, when the Thirteenth returned to their quarters at Garlin, and the Fourteenth went on outpost duty at Tourniquet and Clarac, where they were subsequently relieved by a squadron of the Thirteenth.

On 19th March (after being separated a few days) the two regiments came up with one another again near Vic Bigorre, where Lieutenant-General Sir Thomas Picton with his 3rd Division had forced the enemy from their quarters; and here the brigade once more bivouacked together in a neighbouring wood without baggage or tents, using their cloaks for bedding, after a long march of six leagues and a half. During the night the Heavy Brigade, consisting of 3rd Dragoon Guards and Royal Dragoons,' joined the Light Brigade, and the four regiments formed a division of cavalry under Major-General Fane.

The command of the Light Brigade was given to Colonel Doherty, 13th Light Dragoons, and Lieutenant-Colonel Arthur Clifton of the Royals got command of the Heavy Brigade. At 6 a.m., 20th March, the Cavalry Division proceeded to Tarbes, flanking 20th March the infantry on their right. The cavalry forded the Adour River and was formed in contiguous columns of half squadrons on the opposite bank; the infantry crossed by a bridge.

The enemy now appeared in considerable force, strongly posted on the heights to our front; our infantry attacked. The country was unsuitable for cavalry operations. The enemy was forced and driven from every position by the determined conduct of the British infantry. Our cavalry could only look on and admire their gallant conduct, and when the fight was over bivouacked close by for the night. In the evening the outpost duty was taken by the 14th Light Dragoons.

On 21st March the Light Brigade put up at the village of La Bartha. On 22nd March the affair of St. Gaudens took place. The day was wet, rain poured incessantly. The Fourteenth were in advance, and towards evening put up at a village to the left of the line of route, the Royals in a village to the right, the 3rd Dragoon Guards being halted more to the rear, and the Thirteenth more to the front, near to St. Gaudens, where they distinguished themselves in an engagement with the enemy. On 23rd March a halt was made, and the men endeavoured to clean up after their recent hard work. On 24th March the division proceeded. On 25th the Heavy Brigade, as well as the 14th Light Dragoons, were put up in several adjacent villages, but the Thirteenth occupied one on a different flank.

On 26th March, in pouring rain, the division assembled on the great Toulouse road; the heavies and the 14th Light Dragoons passed the night at the town of Muret, and the Thirteenth went on further, driving the enemy before them along the Toulouse road, through Roques and Portet. On 27th March the Division was halted in villages adjacent to Villeneuve.

On 28th, outposts were established in front of Portet. On 31st the 5th Dragoon Guards came up, and a portion of the Cavalry Division moved on to Mieremont. On 1st April, Villeneuve was occupied. On 4th April the Division was approaching Toulouse, and a chain of outposts was established. On 8th April the 14th Light Dragoons, being in advance, arrived in front of Toulouse, and the other regiments of the Cavalry Division followed. Forage became very scanty and very indifferent in quality. On 10th April, at the Battle of Toulouse, the 14th Light Dragoons acted with the troops under command of Lieutenant-General Sir Rowland Hill, and took part in the battle which ended in the repulse of the French Army, when it was driven off its ground. On the 12th April it was discovered that the enemy had completely evacuated the city of Toulouse in the night.

The Duke of Wellington entered Toulouse in triumph. Our division under Major-General Fane took part in the triumph, and entered the city. Everywhere the British were received by the populace with most joyful acclamations, the white cockade was worn by all, and the white flag was displayed, the air resounded with cries of "*Vivent les Anglais! Vive le Roi!*" After marching through the town the cavalry division crossed a canal, when some of the troops came in contact with portions of the enemy, but the latter retired.

On 13th April news arrived that Napoleon Buonaparte had abdicated, the Bourbon dynasty was restored, and the war was terminated.

On 18th April it was announced in general orders that hostilities were over.

On 22nd our brigade, 13th and 14th Light Dragoons, marched for Aire, and passing through Toulouse halted, the Thirteenth at Tournefuile, the Fourteenth at Columniez. [66] On the 23rd the brigade marched to Isle de Jourdaine, on 24th to Guinat. On 25th April a halt was made; 26th April the brigade marched, the Thirteenth putting up at or near Ordain, and the Fourteenth at Auch.

On 27th April the brigade marched to Vic Fogensac, on the 28th to Vigora, and on the 29th to Aire, where orders were

---

66. Or Colummiez, in Haute-Garonne.

received to continue the march to Mont-de-Marsan,[67] where both regiments arrived on 30th April 1814.'
(*Here the Extracts from the 13th Hussars' Journal end.*)

At Mont-de-Marsan the brigade was broken up. On 13th May the 14th Light Dragoons marched for Bordeaux, and the two regiments, which had served together so long as companions in arms and become such firm friends, were once again separated, and the historic 'Ragged Brigade' became a thing of the past.

Wellington's advance in the middle of February had been much retarded by the late arrival of new clothing for his troops, and as there was no means of transport, he had to send regiments in succession to the stores to fetch it. His first operations were merely to turn the rivers beyond the Nive, at their sources, with Lieutenant-General Sir Rowland Hill's Corps, in which the Fourteenth were acting as advance-guard, being in brigade with the 13th Light Dragoons, now under Major-General Fane's command.

Hill's Corps, consisting of 20,000 combatants and 16 guns, was operating against the left flank of Marshal Soult's army, and took post on the 12th and 13th February about Urcuray and Hasparren. On the 14th they marched in two columns, one by Bouloc,[68] towards the Joyeuse, the other by the great road of St. Jean Pied de Port towards Hellette. Harispe, the French general at the latter town, retired skirmishing towards St. Palais, thus leaving open the great road to St. Jean Pied de Port, while the Joyeuse was passed by the other column.

On the 15th, Hill marched through Meharin upon Garris, but as the road was bad for artillery, the guns went to the right by Armendaritz. Harispe's rearguard was overtaken and driven back fighting.

The affair at Garris ensued: the French general was in position in advance of the Bidouze River on Garris mountain near St. Palais. The fighting began quite late in the day; the 39th and 28th Regiments greatly distinguished themselves, supported by the Spaniards and Portuguese, and the position was carried by the allies, who lost 160 men, but the French losses were 500 men, of whom 200 were taken prisoners.

On the 16th February, Hill crossed the Bidouze, the cavalry and artillery by the bridge at St. Palais, the infantry by the fords.

On the 17th, Hill passed through Domenzain towards the Soissons, meaning to attack the French at Arriveriete, who, under General

---

67. Mont-de-Marsan is in Landes, 65 miles south of Bordeaux.
68. Or Bonloc.

Paris, were defending the Soissons above its confluence with the Gave d'Oleron. [69] The French outposts were driven across the Gave, and the British, 92nd Regiment, took the bridge of Arriveriete, where the allies halted. The French retired; and on the 18th the allies seized the great road running from Sauveterre to Navarrens [70] up the left bank of the Gave d'Oleron. Harispe was reinforced by Generals Paris and Villate, and took up a strong position at Sauveterre, occupying a bridgehead on the left bank, and supported by a brigade of cavalry.

Hill now sent a force up the Soissons to guard the fords, and with Fane's cavalry as well as British and Portuguese infantry spread out between that river and the Gave d'Oleron, he occupied the villages along the road to Navarrens, and opened a cannonade against the Sauveterre bridge-head. After this Marshal Soult sent Pierre Soult with his cavalry brigade and some infantry to operate between Oleron and Pau, fearing that the allies designed to march on the latter place, whilst he decided to hold the Gave d'Oleron and Gave de Pau so long as he could, and then to fall back on Orthes.

By the 23rd February, Wellington had six divisions of infantry and two brigades of cavalry concentrated beyond the Gave de Mauleon on the Gave d'Oleron between Sauveterre and Navarrens. Meanwhile there was a large body of the French army at Orthes and Sauveterre feeling towards Navarrens, and on 24th the allies began to move across the Gave d'Oleron.

On the 25th a large portion of Wellington's army was massed in front of Orthes, including five regiments of cavalry, amongst which were the Fourteenth, whilst another large column with Lord Edward Somerset's brigade of cavalry was at Berenx, five miles lower down the Gave de Pau, and two divisions, as well as Vivian's cavalry, were in front of Peyrehorade; there were also five British regiments at St. Palais, or in that direction.

On the 26th, Marshal Beresford with two divisions and Vivian's Hussar Brigade crossed the Gave de Pau near Peyrehorade, the 18th Hussars having secured the passage of a ford.

On the 27th at daybreak, two more divisions crossed near Berenx by a pontoon-bridge thrown in the night; other portions of the army afterwards crossed, and the French position on the north bank being vigorously assaulted, a fierce battle raged for a considerable time. Hill

---

69. Or Gave d'Oloron.
70. Or Navarrenx, on the Gave d'Oleron, in the Basses-Pyrénées, 12 miles south of Orthes.

with 12,000 men, cavalry and infantry, had remained before the bridge of Orthes, waiting for orders to force the passage of the Gave when a favourable opportunity occurred. At last his opportunity came: he was unable to force the bridge, but forded the river above at Souars, drove back the opposing enemy there, and seized the heights above, cut off the French from the road to Pau, and thus turned the town of Orthes. He then menaced Soult's line of retreat by Salespice on the road to St. Sever, and fell successfully upon his left flank. The Fourteenth shared in these successful operations of the troops under Lieutenant-General Sir Rowland Hill.

In the result the French were completely overpowered and driven from the field. They were pursued by our cavalry and the troops under Lieutenant-General Sir Rowland Hill for a considerable distance, but ultimately escaped across the Adour to St. Sever, Caçeres, and Barcelonne. In this battle Soult lost 4000 men killed, wounded, and taken prisoners, whilst many thousands of conscripts threw away their arms. The pursuit would have been more vigorous had not Wellington himself been wounded above the thigh by a musket-ball which interfered with his riding. The allies lost 2300, of whom 50 with 3 officers were taken prisoners. Besides Wellington, there were also wounded Lord March, afterwards Duke of Richmond, as well as Major-Generals Walker and Ross.

Next day, Wellington continued the pursuit in force. On 1st March, Hill seized the magazines at Aire on the Adour, which river was crossed by the Fourteenth in pursuit on the same day, and on the following day the regiment was engaged in the combat of Aire, when the French were completely repulsed and driven by Sir Rowland Hill's troops from a strong position though fighting with courage and vigour.[71] From this point the enemy retreated unpursued along both banks of the Adour.

It was here that Sergeant Vernor, Private Craig, and Private Rose of the Fourteenth, specially distinguished themselves. As a reward for the gallant conduct of the regiment at the Battle of Orthes, the royal authority was granted in 1820 to bear on its guidons and appointments the word 'Orthes,' and the commanding officer, Lieutenant-Colonel Sir F. B. Hervey, Bart., received another honorary distinction.

On the night of the 7th of March, Marshal Soult sent a body of French troops to Pau with the intention of arresting some nobles, favourable to the house of Bourbon, who were assembled there to welcome the arrival of the Duc d'Angoulême. Major-General Fane

---

71. The above account is taken almost *verbatim* from Napier.

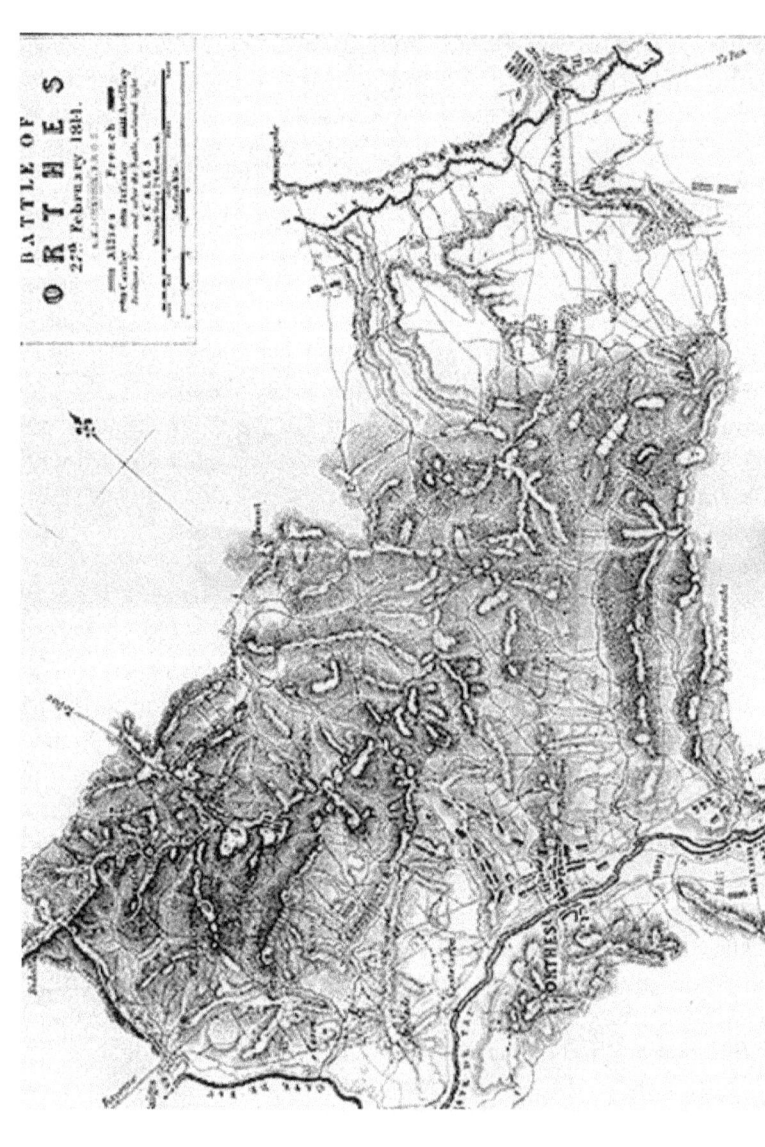

had arrived at Pau with his brigade of cavalry and a strong force of infantry, thus checkmating this movement of Marshal Soult's. The 14th Light Dragoons, with two guns attached, furnished a strong patrol to Pau on 7th, and on the following day (8th March) fell in with the enemy. On this occasion Captain Townsend and four privates were taken prisoners.[72]

In the actions which took place at Aire, 2nd March; Clarac, 14th March; Vic de Bigorre, 19th March; Tarbes, 20th March; and also in some other smaller affairs, the 14th Light Dragoons were engaged with the enemy, and formed the advance-guard of Lieutenant-General Sir Rowland Hill's Corps.

On the 13th March, as well as at Clarac on the 14th March, attacks were made by the enemy; and General Pierre Soult with three regiments of French cavalry moved to Clarac, on the Pau road, to cut off communication with that town and to threaten the right flank of the allied army. The picquet of the 14th Light Dragoons at Clarac repulsed the enemy on the morning of the 14th March, when Captain Babington was unfortunately taken prisoner. On the same evening Captain Badcock, with his picquet, was attacked by the whole of the 5th Regiment of French Chasseurs; he was reinforced by a squadron under command of Captain Milles, and they kept their ground until another squadron under Captain Anderson arrived, when the French were repulsed with considerable loss. Captain Milles was subsequently rewarded with the brevet rank of major for his services on this occasion.

On the 16th March the Fourteenth greatly distinguished themselves in an affair at Castel Paget, where they repulsed an attack of the enemy.

On 18th March the regiment was actively employed in reconnoitring in different directions: the leading squadron, under Captain Anderson, was engaged with the enemy on the Lembege road, the French right was turned by the valley of the Adour, and their outposts were driven back upon Lembege. In this affair Lieutenant William Lyons was killed.[73]

Captain Milles's squadron was attached to the division under the command of Lieutenant-General the Honourable Sir W. Stewart, and was engaged near Vic de Bigorre on the 19th March.

There is a handsome memorial placed in the porch of the English church at Biarritz to the officers and men who lost their lives in the south-west of France during the Peninsular War. It was erected in

---

72 & 73. Cannon's *Record*.

1882, and was visited by Her Majesty Queen Victoria in 1889. The inscription says that 'Lieutenant William Lyons, 14th (King's) Light Dragoons, and one soldier of the same regiment were killed at Vic Bigorre on 19th March 1814.' This is not quite in accordance with Cannon's *Record*, which says Lieutenant Lyons fell on the Lembege road, on the day previously. It is also stated on the Biarritz memorial that one man of the 14th Light Dragoons was killed in action on the 13th March. This may possibly refer to the action at Castel Paget of the 16th March, recorded by Cannon, or to some other affair on 13th March, not recorded.

The British Army had invested Toulouse on 23rd March, but it was not till 10th April 1814 that the action which decided the surrender of the city was fought. The 14th Light Dragoons were present in this battle, serving amongst the troops under Lieutenant-General Sir Rowland Hill in Fane's brigade of cavalry, and they took part in the operations by which the French Army was driven from its ground.

> On the morning of the 14th April, Hill's Division entered Toulouse at 8 a.m., when Fane's brigade of cavalry filed over the great bridge and marched straight through the city, amidst great apparent enthusiasm displayed for the Bourbons and the British army.[74]

Hostilities soon afterwards terminated, and the Emperor Napoleon had already abdicated in favour of the restoration of the Bourbon dynasty.

Thus ended, with glory to the British arms, a war in which the Fourteenth had taken a noble part, and gained seven honorary distinctions, which have since been inscribed on their guidons and appointments, *viz.*

'Douro,' 'Talavera,' 'Fuentes d'Onor,' 'Salamanca,' 'Vittoria,' 'Orthes,' 'Peninsula.'

After leaving Toulouse the Fourteenth marched in brigade with the 13th Light Dragoons towards Mont-de-Marsan, where they arrived on 30th April, and remained for a short time in quarters preparatory to their return to England.

The following copy of the War Office roll of the officers and men of the 14th Light Dragoons, who were among the recipients of the war medal and clasps for the Peninsular campaign, given in the year 1848 by Her Majesty Queen Victoria to the survivors of the wars,

---

74. De Ainslie's *Royal Dragoons*.

was kindly supplied for this book by Major-General the Honourable Herbert Eaton, late Grenadier Guards.

In the list of the officers the rank given below their names is that they held at the time the medals were given in 1848; the other rank (placed immediately after their names) is the rank they held when serving in the Peninsula.

ROLL OF OFFICERS AND MEN OF THE 14TH LIGHT DRAGOONS who were Recipients of the Medal given in 1848 by Her Majesty Queen Victoria to the Survivors of the Wars.

OFFICERS OF 14TH REGIMENT LIGHT DRAGOONS

RANK AND NAME.	Corunna.	Talavera.	Busaco.	Fuentes d'Onor.	Badajos.	Salamanca.	Vittoria.	Pyrenees.	Nivelle.	Nive.	Orthes.	Toulouse.
Jones, William, Captain, Captain H.P. 52nd.		1		1		1		1				
Rofe, Samuel, Paymaster,						1	1			1	1	
Southwell, Hon. A. F., Lieutenant, Lieut.-Colonel H.P. unattached.						1	1			1	1	
Sheil, Theodore, Lt.,			1									
Thursby, John Harvey, Lt.,					1		1	1		1		1
Thomson, Robt., Vet. Surgeon,	1											
Thompson, S. Perronet, Lieutenant, Lieut.-Colonel unattached.									1	1	1	1
Widner, Christopher, Asst. Surgeon, Staff Surgeon unattached.	1	1	1		1	1						
Wainman, William, Captain, Late Brevet-Major.	1	1	1			1	1	1			1	1
Wandesford, Hon. C. H. Butler, Major, Late Hon. C. H. Butler.	1	1										
Anderson, F., Captain, Late Captain.	1					1	1			1	1	1
Babington, John, Captain, Late Lieut.-Colonel.	1	1						1	1	1		
Cust, Hon. Sir Edward, Lieutenant, Lieut.-Colonel unattached.				1	1	1	1	1	1	1		
Clifton, Thomas, Cornet and Lieut.,			1	1								
Douglas, Archibald, Lieutenant, Late Lieutenant.					1		1	1	1	1	1	1
Davies, Daniel Owen, Asst. Surgeon, Surgeon H.P. 18th Foot.[1]				1 1			1			1	1	1
Foster, Augustus, Lieutenant, Late Captain.	1	1				1	1	1				
Gwynne, S., Lieutenant,	1		1		1							
Hawker, Peter, Captain, Lieut.-Colonel.	1											
Humphreys, Charles E., Lieutenant, Lieutenant H.P.						1	1	1	1	1	1	1

[1] Barrossa, in 18th Foot.

Non-Commissioned Officers and Men of 14th Light Dragoons

Rank and Name.	Troop.	Corunna.	Talavera.	Busaco.	Fuentes d'Onor.	Badajos.	Salamanca.	Vittoria.	Pyrenees.	Nivelle.	Nive.	Orthes.	Toulouse.
Cordal, John,		1[1]					1	1					1
Clark, John,							1						1
Giles, John,			1			1		1	1	1	1	1	1
Nicholas, Thomas,			1	1			1	1					1
Wheeler, Benjamin,						1		1	1				1
Brown, Francis,					1		1	1			1		
Benson, Robert,							1	1					1
Bitner, John,								1	1	1	1	1	1
Chambers, Thomas,			1	1	1	1							
Colley, Robert,						1	1	1				1	1
Dry, William,	Capt. Badcock,							1			1	1	1
Darling, John,	Capt. Milne,							1			1		
Dakin or Deakin, John,	Capt. Badcock,							1					1
Elvey, James,			1		1		1	1			1		
Elliott, Elias,	Capt. Townsend,											1	1
Day, Joseph,	Capt. Mills,												1
Fairbairn, And.,	Capt. Badcock,										1	1	
Frake, James,							1	1				1	1
Fisher, George,	Capt. Maerman,						1	1	1	1			1
Forbes, Matthew,												1	1
Hughes, John, Troop Sergt.-Major,			1	1	1								
Hallett, Joseph,			1	1	1	1	1	1	1			1	1
Hainso, John,	F troop,		1	1			1	1	1				1
Jackson, Will.,	Hon. Capt. Capel,		1					1					
Kinghorn, L. Clark,												1	1
Mannering, Henry,								1	1				1
Manton, John,										1		1	1
M'Kay, James,	Capt. Knipe,		1	1	1			1	1			1	1
Moore, Will.,	G troop,		1			1		1	1		1	1	1
Reeves, Joseph,			1	1	1	1	1	1	1			1	1
Randell, John,			1		1		1	1	1				1
Noris, Thomas,	2nd troop,						1	1					1
Silvester, James,	Capt. Brotherton,		1				1	1				1	1
Stone, John,			1				1	1	1	1			
Tilley, George,				1	1	1	1		1			1	1
Wells, Jas., Trumpeter,	D troop,						1	1					1
Clifford, Thos., Sergt.,	Lt.-Col. Hervey,						1	1		1	1		1
Giles, Joseph,	,, ,,						1	1	1		1	1	1
Harrington, Joseph,	Capt. Babington,		1				1	1					
Morris, Thos., Sergt.,				1	1	1	1	1	1			1	1
Smith, John, Sergt.,	Capt. Neville,		1			1	1	1	1	1			1
Shepherd, Sam.,	Capt. Chapman,		1	1	1	1	1		1	1	1	1	1
Smith, Will.,	Capt. Neville,		1	1	1	1	1	1	1	1	1	1	1
Sumner, Geo., Sergt.,	Capt. Sterling,		1	1	1	1	1	1	1	1	1	1	1

[1] Corunna, in royal wagon-train.

NON-COMMISSIONED OFFICERS AND MEN OF 14TH LIGHT DRAGOONS—*Contd.*

RANK AND NAME.	TROOP.	Coruna	Talavera	Busaco	Fuentes d'Onor	Badajos	Salamanca	Vittoria	Pyrenees	Nivelle	Nive	Orthes	Toulouse
Shippey, Thos., Sergt., .	Capt. Sterling	1	1	1	1	1	1	1	1	1	1	1	1
Sactidge, John,							1	1				1	1
Smith, Joshua,	Capt. Deymont,	1	1	1	1	1	1	1					1
Story, Joseph,	Capt. Sterling,	1		1	1	1	1	1			1		
Sims, Isaac,	Capt. Townsend,		1			1	1						
Tuck, John,	Capt. Neville,					1	1						
Topper, Will.,	Capt. Baker,	1		1	1								1
Verner, Alex., Sergt-Major, .	Capt. Badcock,	1	1	1	1	1	1						1
Trower, Will.,	Capt. Kepple,	1	1		1	1							1
Worvall, John,	Capt. Baker,		1						1	1	1	1	
Waddell, Sam.,	Capt. Badcock,	1	1	1	1	1	1	1	1	1	1	1	1
Wooland, Ed.,	Capt. Townsend,	1									1		
Ward, Mathew,	,, ,,	1	1		1		1	1					1
Wood, Arthur,	Capt. Hawker,	1	1	1	1	1	1	1	1	1	1	1	1
Walton, Isaac,	,, ,,	1			1		1						
Westbrook, James,	Capt. Mills,	1	1			1	1				1		
Walter, Robert,	Capt. Smith,			1		1							
Wilson, John, Trumpeter,	Capt. Mills,		1	1									
Young, Jas.,	Capt. Harvey,		1	1		1	1						1
Yates, Jas.,	Capt. Townsend,											1	1
Oliver, Peter, Sergt.,	Capt. Chapman,	1	1	1		1						1	1
Poole, Will.,	Capt. Southwell,								1	1	1	1	
Pridgeon, Thomas,	Capt. Mills,	1			1	1	1						1
Peach, Thomas,	Capt. Brotherton,			1									
Payne, John,	Capt. Mills,	1					1						
Palmer, George,	Capt. Brotherton,	1	1		1		1	1					1
Pain, W. John, Sergt.-Maj., .	Capt. Badcock,		1	1	1	1	1	1	1	1	1	1	1
Powell, Thomas,	Capt. Anderson,		1	1	1	1		1	1	1	1	1	1
Reade, Thos.,	Capt. Mills,	1			1	1							1
Ratcliffe, Jas., Sergt.,		1	1	1	1	1	1	1	1	1	1	1	1
Read, Will.,	Capt. Neville,	1	1										
Rick, Wm.,	Capt. Knight,	1		1		1	1	1					1
Reis, John,	Capt. Mills,	1					1						
Rivers, Richard,	Capt. Anderson,						1						1
Rosier, James,	Capt. Hawkins,	1	1	1	1	1	1	1	1	1	1	1	1
Randle, Thos.,	Lord Manners,	1					1						
Richard, John,	Capt. Townsend,	1				1	1	1					
Rycroft, Wm.,			1				1			1		1	
Smith, Thos., .	Capt. Neville,	1					1			1			
Stone, Thos., .	Capt. Capell,		1		1	1	1	1					1
Summers, John,	Capt. Hawkins,	1	1	1		1	1					1	1
Surman, Thos., Tr. Ser.-Maj., .	Capt. Badcock,											1	1
Kinch, George, Sergt.,	Capt. Hawker,	1	1	1	1	1	1	1	1	1	1	1	1
Lomas, James,	Capt. Knightley,	1		1	1	1	1	1	1				1
Lawrence, Edw.,	Capt. Townsend,		1		1	1	1						
Lomas, Charles,	Capt. Hawker,	1	1	1		1	1	1	1	1	1	1	1
Lane, Richard,	Capt. Brotherton,		1	1	1	1	1						

NON-COMMISSIONED OFFICERS AND MEN OF 14TH LIGHT DRAGOONS—*Contd.*

RANK AND NAME.	TROOP.	Corunna.	Talavera.	Busaco.	Fuentes d'Onor.	Badajos.	Salamanca.	Vittoria.	Pyrenees.	Nivelle.	Nive.	Orthes.	Toulouse.
Measey, James,	Capt. Townsend,	1				1	1						1
Morris, James,	Capt. Knightley,	1	1		1	1	1					1	1
Middleton, Roland,	Capt. Neville,	1	1			1	1	1				1	1
Massey, Joseph,	Capt. Mills,	1					1	1				1	1
Montague, John, L.-Segt.,	Capt. Brotherton,	1	1	1	1	1	1	1	1	1	1	1	1
Marshall, John,	Capt. Milles,	1	1			1	1	1	1				1
Milles, Henry,	Capt. Badcock,						1	1					1
Mackall, Dan., Corp.,	Capt. Babington,	1	1			1	1	1	1				1
Mouldy, Wm.,	Capt. Mills,	1	1	1		1	1					1	1
Mantle, Wm.,	Captain Mahoney,	1		1									
Manning, Chas.,	Capt. Chapman,	1	1	1		1	1	1	1	1	1	1	1
Marner, Jas.,	Capt. Knightley,	1					1	1					
Newman, Wm., Tr. Sergt.-Maj.,	Capt. Chapman,	1	1	1	1	1	1	1	1	1	1	1	1
Dudley, Thos., Tr. Sergt.-Maj.	Capt. Mills,	1	1	1	1	1	1	1	1	1	1	1	1
Duell, Thos.,	Capt. Brotherton,	1											
Darbyshire, Jas.,	Capt. Babington,	1	1										
Davidson, Jas.,	,, ,,	1		1		1	1						1
Davis, Jam.,	Capt. Mills,			1	1		1	1				1	1
Edgers, Edw.,	Capt. Dawson,	1		1	1		1						1
Forrester, David,	Capt. Hawker,			1		1	1	1	1			1	1
Flint, James,	Capt. Babington,						1						
Fulham, John,	Capt. Knight,	1				1	1	1					1
Gibson, Joseph,	Capt. Babington,	1				1	1	1				1	1
Gunn, Will.,	Capt. Wainman,	1	1	1	1	1	1	1	1	1	1	1	1
Groom, Thurlow,	Capt. Badcock,					1	1	1				1	1
Harris, John,	Capt. Baker,	1	1	1	1	1	1	1	1	1	1	1	1
Humphreys, Will.,	Capt. Townsend,	1				1	1					1	
Hanly, W., Tr. Sergt.-Maj.,	Capt. Chapman,	1	1	1	1	1	1	1	1	1	1	1	1
Hicks, Thom.,	A and H troop,						1	1				1	
Heatly, Henry, Trump.-Maj.,	Capt. Baker,	1	1			1	1	1	1	1	1	1	1
Hayelock, Abraham,	Capt. Wainman,	1				1	1	1					
Harrison, George,	Capt. Knight,				1		1	1	1			1	1
Hussey, Thom.,	Capt. Anderson,	1	1			1	1	1					1
Higgs, Joseph,		1	1	1	1	1	1	1	1	1	1	1	1
Ivalts, Henry, Sergt.,	Capt. Chapman,	1	1	1	1	1	1	1	1	1	1	1	1
Jackson, Ab.,	Capt. Badcock,	1	1	1	1	1	1	1				1	1
Jeffery, Rob.,	Capt. Brotherton,					1	1	1	1			1	1
Jevons, Chas.,	Capt. Babington,	1	1	1	1	1	1	1	1	1	1	1	1
Hendley, Chas.,	Capt. Knight,	1						1	1			1	1
Allen, George,	Capt. Mills,									1	1	1	1
Allen, John, Sergt.,	Capt. Chapman,	1	1	1	1		1	1	1			1	1
Anstead, Jas.,	Capt. Neville,	1	1			1	1	1				1	1
Arcote, Dan.,	Capt. Wainman,					1	1	1					1
Bayliss, Thom.,	Capt. Badcock,											1	1
Bevan, Will.,	Capt. Townsend,						1	1					
Branch, Will.,	Capt. Knight,												1

Non-Commissioned Officers and Men of 14th Light Dragoons.—Contd.

RANK AND NAME.	TROOP.	Corunna	Talavera	Busaco	Fuentes d'Onor	Badajos	Salamanca	Vittoria	Pyrenees	Nivelle	Nive	Orthes	Toulouse
Barrett, John,	Capt. Townsend,	1	1	1	1	1	1					1	
Beddy, James,	Capt. Chapman,					1		1					
Benson, Rob.,	Capt. Mills,						1	1					1
Browes, John, Sergt.,	Capt. Brotherton,	1						1					1
Bradshaw, *alias* Bumidge, John, Sergt.,	Capt. Baker,	1	1	1				1	1			1	1
Brazier, Edw.,	Capt. Harvey,							1					1
Barnes, John,	Capt. Baker,					1	1	1	1				1
Butler, Joseph,	Capt. Anderson,	1			1	1	1		1			1	1
Birch, John, Tr. Sergt.-Maj.,	Capt. Baker,						1	1	1		1	1	1
Burke, David,	Capt. Major,	1				1		1	1				1
Bill, John,	Capt. Milles,	1		1			1	1	1			1	1
Barnes, George,	Capt. Babington,							1	1				
Curtis, Rich.,	Capt. Baker,	1		1				1	1				1
Clarke, Walter, Sergt.,	Capt. Knightley,	1				1		1	1			1	
Chase, Henry,	Capt. Mills,	1	1	1									
Casey, Rich., Farrier,	Capt. Hawker,		1	1	1	1	1	1	1	1	1	1	1
Conway, Will.,	Capt. Anderson,									1			1
Connor, James,	Capt. Knipe,	1		1								1	
Craig, Moses,		1		1	1	1	1					1	

Cannon in his *Record of the 14th Light Dragoons* says:—

The 14th (Duchess of York's Own Regiment of Light Dragoons) had acquired a high reputation for the excellent *esprit-de-corps* which pervaded the ranks, and especially for the superior style in which the officers and soldiers had, during several years, performed the duties of picquets, patrols, vedettes, and other services which devolve upon a corps employed in the outpost duty.'

The Fourteenth, under Captain Milles's command, as Lieutenant-Colonel Hervey had obtained leave of absence, remained in quarters at Mont-de-Marsan a short time, and marched on 14th May to Bordeaux, where they were reviewed by Major-General Lord Dalhousie, who highly complimented them for their appearance, discipline, and fitness for further service.

The Fourteenth had been selected, owing to their great reputation acquired in the Peninsular War, from among the other cavalry corps for service in the United States of America; but this order was subsequently countermanded for the present, and on the 10th June they marched from Bordeaux *en route* to Calais, where they embarked on the 15th July and sailed on the 16th for England.

Two troops had remained in England in 1808, and 2 troops had embarked at Lisbon in December 1811, arriving at Portsmouth on the 8th January 1812, and joined the depot. Six troops landed at Dover on the 17th July and marched to the neighbourhood of London.

On the 21st July the Commander-in-Chief, H.R.H. the Duke of York, reviewed 3 squadrons of the regiment on Hounslow Heath, and was pleased to compliment Colonel Sir F. B. Hervey, Bart., on the appearance and efficiency of the several troops.

At the inspection, Cannon relates how the Duke of York said to Colonel Hervey, 'They appear as if they had never been on service.' After the review the 3 service squadrons joined the depot at Weymouth, and were quartered there in Radipole Barracks.

During the five and a half years the regiment had been on foreign service, the non-effectives, including men invalided and sent home, and including horses cast and sold were: 654 men, 1564 troop horses.

Men:—Embarked with regiment	770
Sent from depot to Peninsula	445
Total	1215
Non-effectives	654
Returned with regiment	561
Total	1215
Horses:—Embarked with regiment	720
Remounts	664
Received from other corps	381
Taken from the enemy	63
Spanish	14
Total	1842
Non-effectives	1564
Returned to England	278
Total	1842

The Fourteenth had been on service with the army of the Peninsula under the command of the Duke of Wellington from 23rd December 1808 to 17th July 1814. Since leaving Ireland in 1795 the recruits had been obtained principally by aid parties detached from the regiment to the counties of Worcester, Warwick, Salop, and Berks, with some volunteers received from the Fencible Cavalry in 1800, and from the Royal Wagon Train in 1810. It should be mentioned here that the veterinary surgeon of the Fourteenth, who had held that position since 1801, was Mr. Robert Thompson, and he was succeeded by Veterinary Surgeon Alexander Black on 10th November 1814. Before closing the records of the Fourteenth in the Peninsular War, there are some further interesting anecdotes, written by General Sir T. W. Brotherton, having reference to his experiences with the regiment during this eventful period, which may fittingly find a place here.

ANECDOTES RELATED BY GENERAL BROTHERTON, RELATIVE TO EVENTS WHICH OCCURRED IN THE PENINSULA WHEN SERVING IN THE 14TH LIGHT DRAGOONS, 1808 TO 1814.

1. No army becomes more disorganised and unmanageable, on a retreat, than a British Army! We had several deplorable examples of this in the Peninsula. Sir John Moore's retreat was the first. I did not *belong* to this army, but witnessed its disastrous retreat, being then attached to the Spanish General Marquis de la Romana, when he separated from Sir John Moore the 22nd December 1808, at which time "Corunna Races," as this retreat is appropriately called, commenced. It would be endless to enumerate all that came under my notice on this occasion, besides the hardships that I personally experienced in the rapid and incessant retreat that Romana's army had to make, before the French corps detached to pursue it.

I lost my health through it, and I think was only saved from death by Romana's excessive kindness to me, in literally sharing with me all his comforts. I lived with him, and when I could not get a separate comfortable quarter, he made me sleep in his own room! He was a delightful fellow, and the only Spanish general that the duke speaks highly of, not so much for ability as for integrity and devotedness. He was the man who brought the Spanish army from the north of Germany by stratagem, where they had been most cunningly sent by Napoleon for fear of defection.

2. The soldier who pretends that he never felt fear, is a humbug not to be believed. It is his duty to conceal his feelings as much as possible, however. But there are situations in war so trying to the nerves that the stoutest must feel appalled. I never felt so nervous as I did when I ran the risk of being *hanged* as well as run through the body! I was with the Spanish general, the Marquis de la Romana, in Galicia,

just after his separation from Sir John Moore, and, although our daily operations consisted only in running away whenever the enemy appeared, the *marquis* had thought proper to get manifestoes printed in French, German, Italian, and Spanish, to be distributed amongst the French army to seduce them to desert.

The marshal, Soult, who was following us, highly indignant at this proceeding, which had already caused much desertion from his army, proclaimed that he would *hang* the first person that was taken circulating these papers. One day that we were, as usual, running away from the enemy, I lingered behind with my orderly dragoon, the better to observe the enemy's numbers and intentions, trusting to my good English horse to get away. Accordingly, I remained dismounted till the very last moment, and allowed a few French dragoons to come into the very field where I was, well knowing that, by jumping my horse over one of the stone walls (with which that part of the country is enclosed), I could always bid defiance to them.

But they chased me, and having my pockets full of the proclamation above alluded to, I was desirous of getting rid of them, in case of accidents, and, passing by a ditch, I took them out of my pocket, and tried to throw them into the ditch. It happened, however, to be a very high wind, and they were scattered wide and afar, and picked up by the French. I confess that a thrill of dread ran through my veins, which no danger in action could have produced, perhaps, for to be taken prisoner, and hanged into the bargain, was a contingency of war which I had never contemplated. I escaped, however, with ease, owing to my being so well mounted, but never again carried any such papers about me.

3. When Lord Wellington's headquarters were at Govea, in the north of Portugal, near Castello Branco, and the enemy close thereto, in superior numbers, menacing to enter Portugal again, the 14th Light Dragoons and 1st German Hussars were in front watching the enemy, who, making a sudden movement in advance (in the middle of the night, in order to conceal it from us), but which movement, if not counteracted by a counter movement on the part of our army, would have com-promised its safety, it became urgent that Lord Wellington should be as quickly as possible apprised of it. I was selected to proceed, as quickly as possible, to his headquarters, eight leagues off.

I started on one of my own horses to perform this duty, and naturally chose my *best* horse, a thoroughbred one of great value, which my father had just sent me out from England, having bought him, a colt, at the sale of the King's stud, and broke him in himself, which rendered him of additional value to me. I was obliged to urge him, to perform my important mission, to such a pitch that he dropped under me, when I had reached only halfway to my destination, and I had to get a troop-horse from a cavalry regiment on the road, to conclude my journey, which nearly killed him also.

I reached Lord Wellington's headquarters early in the morning, still dark. They were situated in an old convent; not a soul stirring in the place except the sentry pacing before the gate, who was not a little surprised at my dismounting and knocking loudly at the gate to obtain admittance, which I did with great difficulty and a long delay, and then I had to go on my way in the dark to one of the bedrooms, where I found one of the *aides-de-camp* (the late General Fremantle),[75] and, upon telling him my business (not at first being aware of its extreme urgency), he hesitated as to going to wake Lord Wellington, who, he said, had retired to bed very tired, and in very ill-humour. I said that if I were obliged myself to open the door of his bedroom and wake him, to deliver my message, I must do so, if he would point it out to me.

Fremantle persisting in his refusal to wake Lord Wellington, I actually, myself, went and knocked at the door, and on being admitted, and having delivered my message, Lord Wellington told me to go immediately to Sir George Murray's room (the quartermaster-general) and bring him instantly with me to his room. All was immediately bustle and stir, orderlies and *aides-de-camp* despatched in every direction, and a general movement of the army ordered. It was a most critical moment, and if Lord Wellington had not been apprised of the enemy's movement, to counteract it, our army would have been turned at Castello Branco, the key of Portugal on that side.

The only compensation I received for my valuable horse was £35, the mere regulation compensation. The present Lord Londonderry had offered me 300 guineas for him. I would add that what accounts for Fremantle's scruples about waking Lord Wellington, is the notori-

---

75. Afterwards Major-General Fremantle, C.B., who brought home the duke's despatches from Vittoria and Orthes, as well as the French colours and Marshal Jourdain's baton captured at Vittoria. Captain Fremantle became Adjutant of the Coldstream Guards after the Battle of Talavera, and was *aide-de-camp* to the Duke of Wellington, 1812-16. The latter took him to the Congress of Vienna as he could talk German. He was much liked by the duke, and probably feared him less than the others. General Sir Arthur J. Lyon Fremantle, G.C.M.G., C.B., is his son.

ous fact that his *aides-de-camp* and those about him were all *afraid* of him.

4. However justifiable it might seem that the Spanish and Portuguese *peasantry* should retaliate, revengefully, on the French soldiery for their excessive cruelty and plundering, and though one could not blame them for it or check it altogether, yet, I confess, that to witness their *clergy* joining in these murderous retaliations was revolting, owing to their sacred character. I happened, one day when detached in Portugal to watch the movements of a French column that was winding its way through a most precipitous and rocky part of country, to observe a monk in his ecclesiastical costume (a jolly fellow, resembling Sir Walter Scott's "Friar Tuck," both in character and dress), ensconced *securely* behind a rock, elevated above the road along which the French were marching, whence he could, and did, deliberately take deadly aim at individual French officers and soldiers. He knocked half a dozen over in my presence, and seemed vastly to enjoy the sport, and uttered a ferocious exclamation of joy at each victim he laid low; whilst he, as I before said, was in perfect safety behind an *inaccessible* rock, for the French had not time to dislodge him. The peasantry around gave a wild and ferocious cheer at each deadly shot!

However, making every allowance for *due* revenge, I could not help upbraiding this rascally monk, and I did so on the ground that he was committing a cowardly act, when in perfect safety himself, thus to butcher human creatures, for, after all, nothing can justify, even in war, taking the life of an enemy except in defence of your own. This sanctified character was, however, not only callous to my remonstrances, but even *insolent*, which I could not resent owing to his sacred character, and the blind veneration of the people in this country, even for the *crimes* and immorality of their priests.

5. On Massena's retreat, one day, on following one of their last columns closely, we espied something stuck at the end of one of the men's bayonets, which we at first took to be a loaf of bread, carried as French soldiers usually carry their ration bread, but what was our horror on approaching nearer to find it was a small infant! Incredible atrocity, but too true! The first opportunity we had of communicating verbally with French officers we spoke to them of this revolting fact. They did not deny it, but said it was the deed of an Italian and not a French soldier! What an excuse for such an act, as if every soldier in an army was not equally responsible for such barbarities, or, at least,

for not preventing them.

6. When we were following the enemy towards the Pyrenees we, one day about noon, came up to a bivouac which he had just left. I happened to be in the advance, and on approaching the bivouac, which I expected to find quite abandoned, I heard some loud cries in it, without at first perceiving whence they immediately proceeded. On nearer examination I beheld a man strapped to the stem of a large chestnut-tree, who was roaring most lustily, expecting, I suppose, we should kill him. On approaching nearer I found it to be a negro, and there was a placard, in large letters, over his head with these words, "*Cest un mauvais cuisinier.*" I asked the fellow to explain, and he said he was cook to a French officers' mess of the 53ème de Ligne, "*que les messieurs étaient ce matin de très mauvaise humeur non pas parceque j'ai mal accomodé le dîner mais parceque messieurs les anglais ne leur avaient pas donne le temps de le manger et ils m'ont ainsi traité si brutalement!*"

We naturally thought that no real good cook would have been thus treated, as, in these hard times, such an individual was a precious personage, and we hardly thought it worth trying him. We did, however, and found him an excellent one, but, on the first favourable opportunity, he decamped to the enemy again.

7. The longest ride I ever took, without stopping, was from St. Jean de Luz to Madrid, 95 Spanish leagues (380 English miles). I carried despatches from the Duke of Wellington to the British Ambassador at Madrid, Sir Henry Wellesley, and there were relays of horses ready all the way for me. The most inconvenient and irksome part of the business was that I rode in uniform, and with that most cumbersome of all head-dresses, the bearskin helmet of the British Light Cavalry, at that time. This dress to me was particularly uncomfortable to ride such a distance in, in very hot weather (month of May), as I had been prisoner of war and laid up with wounds since 13th of December, and was quite unaccustomed to such paraphernalia.

8. On a foraging party, in France, at the end of the year 1813, after we had got our forage and were reposing on it, some French peasantry were firing at us, but at such a considerable distance as hardly worth noticing, and here and there a spent ball alighted on us. We were much fatigued, and lying on the bundles of hay which we had foraged in the surrounding country. The orderly dragoon, who was holding my horse and himself lying down, suddenly started up and cried out, "I am wounded!" As he happened to be one of those who are always well

known to their comrades, after a few campaigns, as *rather nervous*, no one attended to him, or believed him, but he kept calling out that he was very much hurt, holding his hand over his right eye.

Knowing the man myself as not worth much, I thought he was making much ado about nothing, and on making him take his hand off his eye, with much difficulty, and perceiving no blood, I felt confirmed in the idea that he was more frightened than hurt. I sent him, however, to the rear, and his wound proved to be not only a most extra-ordinary one but a fatal one. A spent ball had entered the corner of the eye, turned the ball of the eye in its socket without producing a drop of blood, and was taken out at the roof of his mouth. He died of inflammation in forty-eight hours.

9. Nothing could equal the confidence the army felt in Lord Wellington. It was to such a pitch that if it was occasionally separated from him it felt uneasy, for though we had many brave and good generals amongst us, they were, by comparison with him, so immeasurably inferior, in our estimation, that we used to apply to him the famous turf story about the racer "Eclipse," whose owner won an immense stake, at Salisbury races, by taking immense odds that he would not place every horse in a sweepstake, which he did, and won, by placing "Eclipse" first and all the rest of the horses *distanced.*

So it was Lord Wellington might be placed, distancing all generals, either of our own army or of others to which he was opposed. Civilians, in those days, used frequently to put the question to us who we thought ought to replace Lord Wellington if by any chance he were killed or wounded? We were at a loss to answer this question, as we knew of none equal to succeed to such a man, and we were inclined to reply to it by the well-known exclamation of the French soldiers, on the day upon which Turenne was killed by a cannon-shot, and doubt and discussions arose amongst the troops, in the heat of action, as to the man most proper to succeed him in the command.

He, like our chief, had long ridden a favourite horse in all his battles, as Wellington did his favourite "Copenhagen," and, as the army had no very high opinion of the officer entitled, by seniority, to succeed Turenne, they exclaimed, "*Donnez-nous son cheval; il nous mènera à la victoire!*" Turenne was beloved by his soldiers. Wellington was *feared*, but esteemed most highly. He had no winning ways with him, such as are recorded of Turenne and Napoleon, and, above all, he never made speeches to them as Napoleon did, nor did he ever utter those few words attributed to him at the crisis of the battle of Waterloo, "Up, Guards, and at them!"

And as to apostrophising the Pyramids, as Buonaparte did on the field of battle in Egypt, with the famous speech of which the French are so proud, *viz.*, "*Soldats du haut de ces Pyramides vingt Siècles vous regardent!*"—why, our soldiers, instead of being moved by such trash, would have called out "Fudge!" They want no such "blarney" to make them fight, and the less you say to them at such moments, the better. Nothing more than the caution "Steady" is seldom, if ever, wanted in action with British soldiers. Wellington knew this.

10. The severity and peremptoriness of the Duke of Wellington's discipline, on first entering France, was such, that I one day saw a Spanish soldier in the hands of the provost-marshal (the executioner of military justice), leading him to execution, *i.e.* to be hanged on the nearest tree. He seemed to be a fine fellow, with little fear of death at such an awful moment, but only indignant that he should suffer death merely for having taken a fowl out of a farmyard, when he, as he said, had had his father and his mother bayoneted by French soldiers, his sister violated, and his home burnt by them, merely for having joined in the patriotic defence of his country. He was a fine fellow, and his deportment and demeanour on the verge of death was noble. It touched me much, and I would have given the world to have saved him the *ignominious sort of death* that he was to suffer, for his chief horror seemed not so much the fear of *death itself* as the *mode* of it, beseeching as a favour to be shot as a soldier, but not hanged as a felon.

But I knew too well the sternness and peremptoriness of Lord Wellington to presume to interfere. I could not, however bear to see him executed, and turned away from such a dreadful sight.

When in Spain, robbing the beehives of the peasants was a frequent offence, in-spite of Lord Wellington's repeated admonitions and reprimands, and honey was one of the chief profits of the Spanish farmers in some parts. All Lord Wellington's endeavours to stop these depredations having failed, he had recourse to the expedient of keeping whole divisions of the army in which such thefts had been committed "under arms" for days together, sometimes till the delinquent was discovered. This fell hard upon the innocent, and did not often lead to the detection of the thieves.

11. The Duke of Wellington, when in the south of France, anxious to conciliate the inhabitants, and particularly the authorities, re-

ceived a letter from the mayor of a village complaining of his favourite horse having been stolen by some of our people. The duke returned a most polite and lengthy reply, which is recorded in his despatches. The French criticised and ridiculed the duke for paying so much attention to this mayor's complaint, and called it *une niaiserie*. But the duke never wrote a letter which proved of greater advantage to him. This mayor was a most influential person in his district, and was so pleased at the duke's condescension, that in times of great scarcity of provisions and forage he exerted himself, in a most extraordinary way, to feed our troops.

12. *Amateurs*, as they are called in the field, are a description of animal voted a great bore by real soldiers. They consisted of idle gentlemen who must needs try to show their pluck by poking their noses into danger in action (where they had no business to be), till it became too serious to be pleasant, when they immediately decamped, and became objects of derision. They had failed to ascertain the extent of their nerves. In this respect these said *amateurs* differed essentially from the *volunteers* we had with the army, who always recklessly exposed themselves, in order to render themselves conspicuous, as their object was to get commissions given to them without purchase. The largest proportion of these volunteers were killed, but those who escaped were well rewarded for their adventurous spirit.

I have said that these *amateurs* were great bores in the field, and I will mention one glaring instance in the person of a distinguished sailor, though, in one respect, he was a *brilliant* exception to the faults of other amateurs, for when I mention his name, everyone will know that he is the bravest of the brave—Admiral Sir Charles Napier. This distinguished man joined me whilst I was commanding the skirmishers of the rearguard, the day before we retreated on to the position of Busaco. He was most fantastically dressed in his sailor's dress, with a cutlass by his side, a brace of pistols at his waist, etc., looking a strange fellow.

I need not say that he was all day amongst the foremost, but not content with this, he was urging me every moment to charge everything before me; but as I knew my business well, and as doing what he wished would have been contrary to all rule, and orders of Lord Wellington, I told him good-humouredly that he was a bore, and that if he were to go on this way we should realise the Irish story of the "Kilkenny cats," who fought so desperately and perpetually amongst themselves that they were all killed on both sides. Luckily he just after was wounded, and went to the rear, and to my great delight I got rid of him, but was glad he was not seriously wounded.

There were four Napiers in the field at the Battle of Busaco. Sir Charles, the one I have just spoken of, and his three cousins:—Sir Charles, the lamented man just dead; the present Sir William; and last, the present Sir George, three brothers *heroically* brave. The bravery of this family has always been proverbial, and seems hereditary. It was one of their ancestors who invented logarithms. But we unfortunately had a far different race of *amateurs* from the rare specimen I have just adduced in Charles Napier, the sailor, and though one would wish to be charitable towards these would-be heroes, yet I must say they were a great nuisance to the army.

These foolhardy gentlemen who could never be pitied if they got killed or wounded, for having "run into any kind of danger" which they were not bound to encounter, and which appeared to us a sort of vain-glorious vanity, whereas with *us* it was a positive *duty*—were a numerous class who only contributed to *eat our provisions* when scarce, but who suddenly disappeared when things became serious and unpleasant. Mr. L——, whose posthumous memoirs have lately, most injudiciously, been published, was officially employed with the army in the Peninsula, as deputy-judge-advocate. His functions were confined strictly to the closet, and he had no business whatever ever to poke his nose in danger, yet this civil functionary relates the "dangers he had passed," and seems to be proud of them; but he was also a specimen of the genus *amateur*. As this gentleman has thought proper, cursorily, to introduce my name in his memoirs, and in a manner *à propos* to the amateur mania, I will just elucidate this subject by a case in point, in which Mr. L—— is concerned:

He thought fit to come out to the front when some fighting was going on, and happened to hear me exhorting some noble fellows of the Basque peasantry, who were enthusiastic in our favour, but only armed with sticks and scythes, not to expose themselves in this reckless manner, as the French cavalry, with which I was engaged, might occasionally drive us back, and cut up these brave peasants. Mr. L—— very readily took the hint as applying equally to his own precious person, and retreated. But I could not resist the temptation of giving this "quill-driver" my opinion, not only as to the folly of such persons coming, ostentatiously, to the front, but as to the mischievous effect on the morale of troops, by their precipitate retreat when they became frightened, for, though the soldiers heartily laughed at these *amateurs*, yet, at such moments, any-thing that diverts the attention of troops from what ought to be their only object, *viz.* "the enemy," is hazardous.

Mr. L——'s stories of his own adventures are perfectly absurd, except where his *stomach* was concerned, and he is then most in earnest.

13. The guerillas were certainly of great assistance to us, and of great annoyance to the enemy, harassing them continually, but in *battles* they were of little use. They are a very similar force to the Cossacks, and it may be said of them, as Ségur said of the latter, "*Ils ont beaucoup d'audace mais point de bravoure.*"

14. French officers are not very scrupulous as to matrimony. A Spanish lady, at Valladolid, who had a beautiful niece living with her, told me that the *aide-de-camp* of a French general who was quartered in her house, courted this niece, and proposed marriage. The aunt inquired of the general the character of his *A.D.C.*, when the former said:—"I can assure you, madam, that my *A.D.C.* cannot fail to make a good husband, having had much experience in that line, for, to my certain knowledge, he has married in every town we came to, in Spain, for the last three years."!!!

15. Some fulsome French flatterer, who had probably just before licked the dust off Napoleon's feet, said to the Emperor of Russia, just after he entered Paris as a conqueror, on showing him the letter "N," which in compliment to Napoleon had been put on all the public monuments and buildings, "*Sire, il avait des ennemis partout*" (i.e. "*des N mis*" partout), "*Vous, Sire, aurez des amis partout*" (i.e. "*des A mis*" partout).

The famous antique horses plundered from Venice by the French were placed on the triumphal arch at the Tuileries, and there was a chariot attached to them, but no human figure in it, and it was currently understood that, some day, when he expected to have completed his conquests, he (Napoleon) intended his own statue to have been placed there. Another fulsome French flatterer said to the Emperor of Russia, who observed there being no figure in the chariot, "Napoleon, *Le charlatan*" (i.e. "*Le char l attend*").

16. In reference to the event described in General Macdonald's letter, I must observe that, although it has been my lot to have been

engaged in several single combats in the field, during the Peninsular War, yet they were never of my own seeking, but that I was provoked to them by the *braggadocio* manner of the French officers; for I hold it to be very bad taste and feeling to engage *designedly* in these single combats, which in a *mêlée* are unavoidable. War would indeed be more horrible than it is if such individual hostilities were encouraged, which were only suited to a barbarous age.

For the sake of example, an officer cannot well decline a challenge to single combat offered in the bullying manner with which the officer commanding the French regiment of dragoons bore himself towards me on this occasion. Generally, the skirmishing of the cavalry in the Peninsula used to be carried on in the most chivalrous manner, I had almost said *amicable* manner, sometimes even the officers of both parties *shaking hands* before commencing; and often have we drank a glass of wine together *after* the day's fight was over!

In this instance there was a coarse, bullying manner in the French officer which made me wish to chastise him, but I was on a very small Spanish horse, not much higher than fourteen hands, whilst he was, in all points, a formidable antagonist, *in appearance*, mounted on an immense horse—a very large, powerful man himself, with an immense fur cap—in short, looking as savage as a dragoon could look. My own men and General (then Captain) —— tried to dissuade me from encountering this *Goliath*, but I could not stand his taunts, and rode at him on my little charger, intending to equalise the combat through the agility of my little horse, in compensation for the great weight of my antagonist.

He did not, however, wait for me, but, just before I came up to him, he turned his horse and retired amidst the yells and hisses, not only of *my* own men and the British officers present, but of *his* own men also, and, although I found myself alone amongst the latter, not only did they not attempt to cut at me or even to interrupt my return to my own troops, but showed me every mark of respect and approval of my conduct, by cheering me and waving their swords.

Sir Andrew Leith Hay, in his book,[76] describes a very different affair of this sort, in which I was engaged, and in which I met a most chivalrous, fine young fellow of a French officer, and I have never ceased to lament having wounded him so seriously as to have caused his death, but in this instance, likewise, I have the consolation that it was not of my own seeking, but a determined challenge on the part

---

76. *Narrative of the Peninsular War* by Andrew Leith Hay also published by Leonaur.

of my opponent in front of the line of battle.

This alone can, in my opinion, excuse a single combat in war, or its being accidental in a *mêlée*.

17. I had nine horses shot under me during the Peninsular War. This is not a great number considering the constant exposure to fire. When a horse has once been hit by musketry, ever after he trembles under fire, as if by instinct. It may be my fancy, but I have always thought I perceived this.

18. In a regiment which has been long in the field, and frequently in action, not only are the officers well known by the men, but every individual is known to each other, reciprocally. Thus I knew to a nicety what each officer and private in the 14th Light Dragoons was worth, and what he was fit for. One of the indifferent ones in action, well known to his comrades as such, in my squadron, being one day in the front rank, when we were advancing to charge a French squadron opposite to us, cut his horse's head almost in two at the moment he thought we were about to come in contact with the enemy. The enemy, however, turned just before we reached him, thus exposing the man's trick.

19. It was once reported to me, when we were formed up and exposed to a severe fire, that a man in my squadron had exclaimed—"This is murder, it is too bad to leave us here." As this speech was calculated to dishearten the men, I thought it advisable to make an example of the man at the moment, instead of bringing him to trial afterwards, and I called him out of the ranks and took him to the most exposed spot I could find, where I thought a cat with nine lives could not live for a minute. I left him there, and told him to stop there as a vedette. The balls fell thick about him, but he escaped them all as if by a miracle, whilst his comrades in the ranks fell fast. Such is the fatality in action, verifying the soldier's saying, "*Every bullet has its billet.*" To my great disappointment this cowardly rascal escaped unhurt. The proceeding, however, had its desired effect, for the men seemed delighted at it.

20. In one of our sharpest skirmishes it was reported to me, by one of the men, that a sergeant was showing a very bad example, and, instead of exposing himself, like others, to the fire of the enemy, he was skulking repeatedly behind the large cork trees, and on my notice being directed towards one of these trees I saw the sergeant hiding

himself behind. In the moment of indignation I rode up to him, and licked him as long as I could stand over him, with the flat of my sabre, and ordered him out of the field.

After this chastisement, I could not have tried him by a court-martial for cowardice, but I might myself, if he had chosen to come forward against me, have got into a scrape, for the proceeding on my part was certainly hasty and irregular, but he knew too well that if he complained, although I might have been reprimanded, he would have been the more shamefully exposed.

He asked for his discharge, and left the regiment.

After leaving the service, one might have supposed that this man would have shown spite and revenge, but he felt conscious that the infliction of the punishment was merited, for I met him often, after our return to England, in the streets of London, when he always saluted me most respectfully. He had become a schoolmaster, and was well qualified for the situation, as he was an excellent scholar.

21. On the occasion of erecting a monument to one of my old comrades, Colonel Townsend[77] of the 14th Light Dragoons, and introducing on it the Prussian Eagle on the helmet, which the Fourteenth wore in those days, because the regiment was the "Duchess of York's Own" (who was a Prussian princess), I am reminded of a curious little incident which occurred to me through wearing this regimental badge.

When attached to the Spanish general, the Marquis de la Romana, in Galicia, just after he had separated from Sir John Moore, I was one day traversing a narrow defile, with my orderly dragoon behind me, when I was suddenly assailed by a volley from half a dozen muskets, which wounded my orderly's horse, and one ball went through my helmet without hurting me. Being in a part of the country where I knew the peasantry to be friendly to our cause, and hostile to the French, I was at a loss to account for this extraordinary proceeding, seeing at the time the peasants on the top of a rock, who had fired at me. In a moment after, however, I was surrounded by several hundreds of these armed peasants and ferociously assailed by them, seemingly with a determination to despatch myself and my orderly.

I was at this period but little acquainted with the Spanish language, as this occurred at the end of 1808, and we had not then been long in the country, but I could understand sufficiently to know that the

---

77. Colonel Townsend died in Ireland in 1845.

eagle on our helmets was the cause of it all. They mistook it for the French eagle, to which it is very similar, and had it not been for a friar who was amongst these peasants, and armed as they were, and apparently their leader, we should probably in one more instant have been sacrificed by this infuriated rabble. Fortunately he spoke French, and on my explaining to him that I was an English officer, and that the eagle was the Prussian eagle and not the French, he, though with some difficulty, persuaded the peasants of the fact, and we were released and allowed to proceed.

Never had I a narrower escape than on this occasion. Guns and pikes, etc. etc., were put close to my body with a view of putting an end to me, and my orderly dragoon, a fine, brave fellow, was so exasperated at seeing me thus in peril, that he made the matter worse, and nearly caused my instantaneous death, by drawing his sabre and cutting right and left at my assailants.

I was taken to the prison at Lamego till my passport was sent to Oporto to be verified; and it was returned with an order from the Bishop for my release. Maréchal Beresford (now Lord Beresford), on being informed of the following conduct of a little American settled as a watchmaker at Lamego, had him sent for a long period to prison, till I interceded for him. This little wretch was employed by the mob, who doubted my being an Englishman, to ascertain, by conversing with me, whether I was or not; and he, with all the low spite of a Yankee, swore that I was not, and that I could barely speak English, when the mob again wanted to put me to death as a spy, and were only prevented by the courageous friar who had before saved my life. I must explain, in elucidation of the above story, that the Bishop of Oporto at this date was a very powerful personage in the north of Portugal, and governed it like a king. He was an intriguing, artful priest, and hated the English as heretics.

******

The two following anecdotes of General Brotherton's do not refer to his service in the 14th Light Dragoons, but to the time when he served in Egypt as a young officer in the Coldstreams, in the army under General Sir Ralph Abercromby, in 1801, but their great military interest must excuse their insertion here.

******

1. The first time I was under fire was when carrying one of the colours of the Coldstreams in Egypt, the battalion marching in line.

The sergeant behind me (called the covering sergeant), seeing me a raw youth, then only sixteen years of age, said in a respectful but half-joking way, "How do you feel, sir?" to which I replied, "Pretty well, but this is not very pleasant:" the men were falling fast. The sergeant, who was a seasoned veteran, liked the reply, for he seemed to take me under his special protection and care ever after. His name and appearance I shall never forget.

It was Sergeant Stuckey—I often went to Chelsea to see him, where he died at the age of eighty-four, about the year 1840. Probably, had I pretended to feel quite at my ease, and to despise the danger altogether, the shrewd old sergeant would have put me down as a "humbug." It was this same sergeant who, along with poor Beckett, assisted me in the water, when a shell sunk the boat, to the westward of Alexandria.

2. When part of the army moved to the west of Alexandria, we had to embark in flat-bottomed boats on a lake. I was carrying one of the colours of the Coldstreams, and Beckett (afterwards killed at Talavera) the other. He, poor fellow, was a very tall man—six feet two or three, I think. We were shelled by the enemy, and one shell fell in the boat, took off the legs of two men, and sunk it. The lake was very shallow, so much so that Beckett stalked along, walking with his colour in his hand, with water just up to his chin. I had to swim and carry my colour, which was no easy job; but I would have died, of course, sooner than let it go.

Beckett, who was a delightful, good-natured fellow, stuck to me and assisted me all he could, but shell and shot fell thick around and many men suffered from them and were drowned. I was fortunate enough, however, to reach the shore with my colour, and we drove the enemy before us. It is singular that Beckett met with nearly a similar adventure on the landing in Egypt, two months before, and then had to swim for it, with the colours in his hand.

Services of General Brotherton.

General Sir Thomas William Brotherton, G.C.B., the author of the above anecdotes of events in the Peninsular War, entered the army as an ensign in the Coldstreams in January 1800, became Lieutenant and Captain, July 1801; Captain in the 14th Light Dragoons in 1807; Major, November 1811; Lieutenant-Colonel by brevet, 19th May 1814; served in the Fourteenth till 1820, retired on half-pay same year; obtained the rank of Colonel, 22nd July 1830, and was appointed *aide-*

de-camp to the King. On 8th February 1832 he became *commandant* of the Cavalry Depot at Maidstone. He was promoted to the rank of Major-General, 23rd November 1841, and on 17th August 1842 was appointed to the staff of the Northern District at York. On 1st January 1847 he became Inspecting-General of the Cavalry in Great Britain; was promoted Lieutenant-General on 11th November 1851, and General on 1st April 1860. He was made K.C.B. in 1855, and G.C.B. on 28th June 1861.

He served under General Sir Ralph Abercromby in Egypt in 1801; in Germany under Lord Cathcart in 1805 5 an d m Portugal, Spain, and France during the whole of the Peninsular War, from 1808 to 1814. For his services he received the war medal with seven clasps, for the battles of Busaco, Fuentes d'Onor, Salamanca (where he was wounded), Vittoria, Pyrenees, Nivelle, and Nive, in which last battle he was again wounded and taken prisoner. Besides these battles he was present at all the cavalry affairs and skirmishes in which his regiment, the 14th Light Dragoons, was engaged, and was at the action on the Coa. He was several times wounded in these skirmishes. He died in January 1868.

The contest in North America, which had been recommenced in 1813, was still going on; and on the 31st August, 2 troops of the Fourteenth, followed by 2 troops on the 10th October, dismounted, sailed from Portsmouth and Plymouth respectively, one party arriving at Jamaica on 24th November. Here an expedition was assembled under Major-General (afterwards Lord) Keane for an attempt on New Orleans, on the River Mississippi, no miles from the Gulf of Mexico. The expedition arrived off the coast of Louisiana on the 10th December, where the troops had to be landed in light vessels and open flat-bottomed boats to navigate Lake Borgne, and then to traverse a difficult morass before approaching the enemy's works.

The Americans opposed in such overwhelming numbers, having extensively fortified lines and batteries as well as armed vessels on the river, that the enterprise failed and had to be relinquished. [78]

The first squadron of the Fourteenth arrived in the Mississippi River on the 27th December 1814, and the second squadron on the 5th January 1815. On the 2nd January 1815 a third squadron embarked for North America, but afterwards rejoined the regiment at Hounslow, and remained in England.

Major T. W. Brotherton became Brevet Lieutenant-Colonel on the

---

78. Cannon's *Record*.

19th May 1814, and also received the Companionship of the Bath; and Major C. Baker became Brevet Lieutenant-Colonel on the 4th June 1814. At this period the uniform still remained blue, with orange facings and silver lace.

1815

Two squadrons in the second attack on New Orleans under Sir A. Cochrane, on the 8th January, the two squadrons served dismounted. Major-General the Honourable Sir E. Pakenham, K.C.B., was killed. Major-Generals Gibbs and Keane were dangerously wounded, when the command of the troops devolved upon Major-General Lambert, who in his despatch to Earl Bathurst, dated off Chandeleur Island, 28th January 1815, states:—

> The conduct of the two squadrons of the 14th Light Dragoons, latterly commanded by Lieutenant-Colonel Baker, previously by Major Milles, has been the admiration of every one, by the cheerfulness with which they have performed all descriptions of service.
>
> P.S. I regret to have to report that during the night of the 25th, in very bad weather, a boat containing Lieutenant Brydges and Cornet Hammond with 37 men of the 14th Light Dragoons unfortunately fell into the hands of the enemy, off the mouth of the Rigolets. I have not been able to ascertain correctly the particular circumstances.—(*London Gazette Extraordinary*, 9th March 1815.)

The troops returned to the fleet, and this was the occasion on which the boat with 2 officers and 37 men of the regiment fell into the hands of the enemy, as related above. [79]

The four troops left the Isles Dauphins for England on the 23rd March. They anchored at Spithead on the 13th May, landed at Portsmouth on the 14th, 15th, and 16th May, and marched to join the remainder of the regiment at Hounslow, whither the depot had moved from Radipole Barracks, Weymouth, two months previously, detaching 50 rank and file with officers and non-commissioned officers to Hampton Court Barracks.

On the 6th April the Fourteenth received an intimation from

---

79. The Regimental Digest of Services has the following entry:—'1815. January 19th and 21st. At the disembarkation near New Orleans to land at Cat Island, Lieutenant Brydges, Cornet Hammond, 1 troop sergeant-major, 39 rank and file captured by enemy.'

H.R.H. the Commander-in-Chief stating that H.R.H the Prince Regent had been pleased, in the name and on behalf of H.M. King George III, to grant them permission to bear the word 'Peninsula' on their guidons and appointments, in commemoration of their distinguished services in Portugal, Spain, and France, from 1808 to 1814.

Napoleon Buonaparte having quitted Elba on 26th February 1815, returned to France and once more regained the throne as Emperor. War accordingly began afresh, and ended in the glorious victory at Waterloo. As two squadrons had been employed in the Mississippi, and a third had embarked on 2nd January for the same destination, the Fourteenth were unfortunately prevented taking any part in that action and in the operations on the continent which preceded it; but two of their officers, Colonel Sir F. B. Hervey, Bart., and Major the Honourable H. Percy, served on the personal staff of Field-Marshal the Duke of Wellington in the Battle of Waterloo. [80]

The *London Gazette*, dated 22nd June 1815, states as follows:—

Major the Honourable H. Percy arrived late at night on 21st June, in London, with a despatch from Field-Marshal the Duke of Wellington, K.G., to Earl Bathurst, His Majesty's Principal Secretary of State for the War Department, about the victory gained at Waterloo (dated 19th June 1815).

In this the Duke of Wellington says:—

I send with this despatch two eagles taken by the troops in this action, which Major Percy will have the honour of laying at the feet of His Royal Highness. I beg leave to recommend him to your Lordship's protection. I have the honour, etc.

            (Signed)   Wellington.

The third squadron alluded to above, which sailed from Portsmouth, 2nd January, for North America, proceeded first to Cork to join the reinforcements, for same destination, collected there under Major-General Johnstone. The order, however, was countermanded, and the two troops 14th Light Dragoons returned from Cork to England, landed at Deal on 30th March, were detained a short time at Canterbury, and thence went to Hounslow.

The regiment left Hounslow on 30th December for Bristol, under Major and Brevet Lieutenant-Colonel Baker, where they embarked in various parties at intervals up to 31st January 1816, and proceeded to

---

80. Cannon's *Record*.

Ireland, landing at Waterford and Cork.

Eight farriers were for the first time appointed to be borne on the strength of the regiment in December, and the troops were reduced from ten to eight: total strength, exclusive of officers, being 677, and troop-horses, 581. The eight troops were designated by the numbers 1 to 8, according to the seniority of their captains.

1816

On the 1st January and following days the regiment landed at Cork and Waterford, and proceeded to Dundalk, the last detachment disembarking in February.

All the front peaks of the troop saddles of Light Cavalry were cut down on the 24th September, and a further reduction in the establishment of the Fourteenth also took place, the total strength of non-commissioned officers and men being 509, with 333 troop-horses.

One lieutenant-colonelcy was reduced, and in the Army List for 1817, Colonel Sir F. B. Hervey, Bart., is the only lieutenant-colonel of the Fourteenth, Major-General S. Hawker having been removed from that position, which he had occupied since 1800, with the exception of a short interval only (1802-3) when he was temporarily on half-pay.

1817

Further small reductions took place in the 8 troops; 1 lieutenant only was allowed per troop from 27th January. The Fourteenth remained stationed at Dundalk.

1818

Still further reductions were made in the numbers of the various ranks of the regiment, but the number of the troops remained eight. By an order dated Dublin Castle, 23rd October 1818, each troop was to have only 2 sergeants, 3 corporals, 1 trumpeter, 1 farrier, 42 privates, 34 troop-horses.

On the 25th December, Captains Townsend and Badcock were promoted to the rank of major in the army for their services in the field during the war in the Peninsula, and a second assistant-surgeon ceased to be borne on the establishment of the regiment.

In July the Fourteenth moved to Portobello Barracks, Dublin, to be quartered. During its stay in Ireland the regiment received on several occasions the thanks of both Major-General White and Major-General Sir T. Sidney Beckwith for its good conduct, discipline, and efficiency.

On the 27th May, General Sir George Beckwith, G.C. B., Commander-in-Chief in Ireland, formed up the regiment, in column of half squadrons, in Dublin, and personally complimented all ranks for their excellent conduct and discipline during the period of their stay under his command in Ireland.

1819

The total establishment of the Fourteenth was now fixed at
- 8 Troops.
- 28 Officers (5 Staff Officers).
- 404 Non-commissioned officers and men.
- 273 Troop-horses.

In June they embarked at Dublin, and landed at Liverpool 11th June, having crossed the Channel in vessels named the *Duke of Leinster*, *Duke of Richmond*, *Shamrock*, and *Dauntless*. From Liverpool there was a long march to the south of England.

Major-General Sir Robert Bolton, Inspector-General of Cavalry, inspected the regiment in June at Camberwell, a halt being made for two days on the march. After 200 miles' march along the roads there were no sore backs, and the major-general reported favourably on the well-regulated and established discipline which pervaded all ranks. The Fourteenth proceeded thence to Canterbury.

Whilst stationed at Canterbury the various troops of the regiment were much scattered through Kent, at Deal, Hythe, Dover, Ringwould, Folkestone, Romney, Lydd, Sandgate, and Highgate, small parties being detached to these various places and employed in assisting the Riding Officers of the Revenue.

On 26th August, 2 squadrons went from Canterbury to Chatham, returning on 7th September.

On 22nd September, 5 troops left Canterbury and proceeded as follows:—
- 1 Troop to Ipswich.
- 1 Troop to Bury St. Edmunds.
- 1 Troop to Lynn.
- 2 Troops to Norwich, and detachment to Yarmouth in relief of the 9th Lancers.
- 1 Troop and headquarters remained at Canterbury,
- 1 Troop at Hythe.
- 1 Troop at Deal.

In December the 2 troops at Deal and Hythe joined headquarters at Canterbury.

On 31st July, blue-grey kersey wove overalls were taken into wear by all ranks.

On 24th September, Colonel Sir Felton B. Hervey, Bart., C.B., Commanding the Fourteenth, and Secretary to the Master-General of the Ordnance, died. His loss was most deeply deplored by the whole corps.

Brevet Lieutenant-Colonel Baker succeeded Sir F. B. Hervey as Lieutenant-Colonel of the Fourteenth on 30th September, and Brevet-Major T. P. Milles became Major in succession. Lieutenant-Colonel Baker had practically had command of the regiment for some time already in the absence of Sir Felton Hervey on staff employment.

1820

On 17th January, His Majesty's royal permission was granted to the Fourteenth to wear on its guidons and appointments the words:—

'Talavera,'
'Fuentes d'Onor,'
'Salamanca,'
'Vittoria,'
'Orthes.'

The letter containing the intimation to the regiment of the royal permission for these additional honours was signed 'Harry Calvert, *Adjutant-General*, Horse-Guards, 15th March 1820.'

On 24th June the Fourteenth were inspected at Canterbury by Major-General Lord Edward Somerset. The men had lately been employed in the flat marshy ground near Romney, and many were sick with ague and similar complaints. Vaccine inoculation was regularly practised in the hospitals at this period. The review report states that there was a *Riding-Master* now in the regiment, but his name does not appear in the Army List amongst the roll of officers until the year 1823. Four men per troop were taught how to shoe horses on an emergency.

In June the 5 troops which were in Norfolk and Suffolk rejoined headquarters at Canterbury, and the Fourteenth again furnished detached troops to Deal and Hythe for revenue services.

On 19th July a squadron was sent from Canterbury to Dover on civil duty.

On 31st July, 4 troops and headquarters left Canterbury for Brighton.

On 14th August a squadron left Dover for Lewisham, and at the same time a squadron moved from Brighton to Reigate, *en route* to Richmond.

It appears from the general marching orders of this period that 6 troops were at Richmond, Putney, Mortlake, etc., early in September, and were ordered to march about 10th September to Brighton in two divisions, and that they arrived at Brighton, 13th September, where the 85th Regiment (Duke of York's Own Light Infantry) arrived from Richmond, Twickenham, etc., on 15th, 16th, and 18th of the same month. It also appears from same marching orders that the 6 troops of the 14th Light Dragoons left Brighton again on 30th September for the above-named places in the vicinity of London, and part of the regiment was employed at Richmond in September and October, and at Wimbledon in October, when it was again inspected by Major-General Lord Edward Somerset, Inspector-General of Cavalry.

There appears to have been a new system of military equitation introduced about this period, and the Fourteenth were temporarily cantoned during the autumn months about Richmond and Wimbledon, having come there from Kent and Brighton, and afterwards returned about October to Brighton, sending detachments to places along the coast of Sussex. Major and Brevet Lieutenant-Colonel T. W. Brotherton went on half-pay on 25th September, and Brevet Lieutenant-Colonel the Honourable Henry Percy, C.B., who had served on the Duke of Wellington's staff at Waterloo, became Major on the 12th October.

www.ingramcontent.com/pod-product-compliance
Lightning Source LLC
Chambersburg PA
CBHW021003090426
42738CB00007B/632